Kagame's
Killing Fields

Kagame's Killing Fields

David Himbara

ISBN: 1546607285
ISBN-13: 9781546607281
Library of Congress Control Number: 2017907860
CreateSpace Independent Publishing Platform
North Charleston, South Carolina

Contents

Main Argument

———

RWANDA HAS REMAINED AN EXCEPTIONALLY violent place since the 1990s. The 1994 genocide gave way to a slow-motion loss of lives, the effects of which linger twenty-three years later. Hundreds of thousands of Rwandans died or mysteriously disappeared at the hands of the state. No social strata escaped the state-sponsored killings—religious leaders (including bishops), political leaders, military officers, businesspeople, journalists, community leaders, citizens, and even a personal physician to the Rwandan head of state perished. The man at the center of this violence is Rwanda's president, Paul Kagame.

My argument in *Kagame's Killing Fields* is that besides becoming synonymous with serial extrajudicial killings, disappearances, and massacres, Kagame delights in violence. His ferocious public rhetoric gloats in the physical violence that accompanies the actual killings, safeguarding Kagame's absolute power in two ways. First, the violence has to be so immensely brutal as to deter would-be challengers to his power. Since 1994, Rwandan and Congolese civilians have realized that Kagame means business; they mostly preferred acquiescence to brutal punishment. Second, a scapegoat has to take the blame. Kagame is a master at scapegoatism—he can never go wrong.

In this terrifying environment, Kagame, too, unwittingly became a victim of his own intimidation techniques. Ferocity became the norm, leading to irrational decisions and a vicious cycle of senseless killings that further exposed his dependence on violence. Kagame's genius is in branding himself a visionary champion of African peace and prosperity while simultaneously conducting a campaign of terror that has claimed more lives than the combined mass murder by all other contemporary African dictators. Kagame's manipulative brilliance is further demonstrated by the constitutional amendment he engineered to guarantee himself immunity from persecution for serious crimes once he is no longer head of state.

Kagame is by no means the first to use violence as a means of accumulating power in Rwanda. Violence and genocide were embedded in the politics of Kagame's two predecessors. Both Grégoire Kayibanda, who ruled Rwanda from 1962, and Juvenal Habyarimana, who overthrew Kayibanda in 1973, used violence and genocide as power. A political psychology of violence transcends individual power incumbents in Rwanda. The difference is in the scale of savagery, with Kagame exporting violence even beyond Rwandan borders to the Democratic Republic of Congo (DRC) and other countries.

Author Biography

——

DAVID HIMBARA IS AN EDUCATOR and development strategist as well as an author. He has worked in several countries, including Canada (where he studied), the United States, South Africa, Kenya, and Rwanda. He is currently a scholar in residence and professor of international development at Centennial College in Toronto, Canada. His current professional passion is fighting energy poverty in sub-Saharan Africa (SSA), where more than 620 million out of SSA's population of one billion have no electricity. One of Himbara's major accomplishments was coaching governments in eastern and southern Africa in evidence-based policy making as part of Knowledge Management Africa. He taught and performed strategic work at the University of the Witwatersrand (Wits) in various capacities from 1994 until 2013 when he returned to Canada. While in South Africa, Himbara led a team that succeeded in bringing the World Bank's Center for Learning on Evaluation and Results (CLEAR) to Wits. CLEAR supports governmental clients throughout Africa in evaluating and monitoring capacity development.

Another career highlight was leading and working with the teams that conducted South Africa's ten-year review of achievements and challenges in democratic governance. Himbara also served as a consulting team leader for several development agencies, including the African Development Bank, and as a strategist for the United Nations Development Program. While in South Africa, Himbara worked alongside leadership at the Central University of Technology to craft strategies for reforming decision making and implementing the university's Vision 2020.

A Rwandan-Canadian, Himbara saw President Paul Kagame's policies and personality up close. Himbara worked for Kagame twice, from 2000 to 2002 and from 2006 to January 2010. During the latter tenure, he set up and headed the Strategy and Policy Unit. In that capacity, Himbara was founding chairperson of the Rwanda Development Board and the Institute for Policy Analysis and Research. He was also chairperson of the World Bank–funded Human and Institutional Development Agency.

Himbara holds a Ph.D. in political economy from Queen's University in Kingston, Ontario, Canada. He is widely published in major journals and online. He is also the author of *Kenyan Capitalists, the State, and Development* and *Kagame's Economic Mirage.*

Preface

————

THIS WORK BEGAN AS A response to critics of my earlier book, *Kagame's Economic Mirage*, published in June 2016. While my readers appreciated the economic analysis, they maintained that the book did not go far enough in scrutinizing Kagame's political violence. This subject, they argued, also deserves to be analyzed through the evidence-based method of *Kagame's Economic Mirage*. The critics also pointed out— correctly, I think—that the political violence that continues to ravage Rwanda is often subjected to partisan, emotional writings that do not document the extent and intensity. *Kagame's Killing Fields* is my attempt to meet this challenge.

There was, however, one daunting difficulty. I had to figure out where to find hard evidence. In fields such as economics, data and reports are regularly published by governments and international organizations, but there is no equivalent in politics, least of all in the documentation of political violence. Further, the domestic and international nongovernmental organizations (NGOs) that provide such data under normal circumstances operate in an extremely hostile environment in Rwanda. In fact, NGOs hardly exist in Rwanda, given the immense violence targeting domestic researchers and the consistent denial of research visas for their international counterparts.

These difficulties notwithstanding, I acquired valuable primary resources that enabled me to write this book, composed of documentary evidence from official records. For the genocide period, I sought to gain unfiltered access to Kagame through his speeches, interviews, and correspondence between the Rwandan Patriotic Front (RPF) and the United Nations Security Council. The US government's declassified documents and the United Nations' archived materials add some useful insights into Kagame's views at the height of genocide. For the postgenocide phase, I draw mainly from three official sources: the government of the United States, the government of Rwanda, and the United Nations' agencies. The Rwandan case studies by the United Kingdom Foreign and Commonwealth Office also provide useful insights. By far, the annual human-rights reports of the US Department of State comprise the most detailed and consistent documentation of Kagame's atrocities. Together with the US Department of Defense, the State Department also publishes annual reports on foreign military training funded by the American government. These reports shed light on the role of the United States in building Kagame's military. Additionally, the US Congressional testimonies by senior American government officials are rich sources. In the case of Rwanda, I scrutinize the government's reports, including those of the Rwanda National Commission for Human Rights (RNCHR), and I review Kagame's statements and his government's responses to charges of violence at home and abroad. I also consulted various documents of the United Nations Human Rights Commission, to which Rwanda periodically reports.

I must make a disclaimer here. I worked for Kagame from 2000 to 2002 and from 2006 to 2010. Admittedly, I was ignorant of the military side of the Rwandan state, as my work dealt with developmental policy and economic reforms. I use no anecdotal insights I may have gained from my Rwandan experience. Coincidentally, the period in which I worked for the Rwandan president was relatively free of violence.

This book is organized chronologically, beginning with the contextual background in chapter 1 followed by the Rwandan genocide in 1994, which is the subject of chapter 2. In scrutinizing Kagame's role, we see a scheming operator gambling with people's lives for the sake of achieving absolute power. Chapter 3 reviews Kagame's killing fields inside Rwanda since 1994, illustrating the pattern and scale of systemic repression, disappearance, and death for thousands of Rwandans.

Chapter 4 analyzes Kagame's killing fields in DRC. Besides reviewing Kagame's role as the principal occupying power and his wars against Uganda deep inside the DRC, we scrutinize how Kagame used a legal procedure at the

International Court of Justice to avoid trial for crimes against humanity. We also see the implications for the codefendant, Uganda, which faced trial and lost.

Chapter 5 deals with Kagame's confrontations with his African counterparts about harassment and assassinations of members of the Rwandan diaspora on foreign territories. The outcomes of these conflicts ranged from the expulsion of Rwandan diplomats to the closure of Rwandan diplomatic missions. I also consider how Kagame's death threats reached critics as far abroad as the United Kingdom and Sweden.

Chapter 6 examines the responses to Kagame's killing fields by his main donor and diplomatic supporter—the United States. We see how each American administration, from Bill Clinton to George W. Bush to Barack Obama, handled the Kagame factor. The relationship is characterized by a persistent contradiction. On the one hand, the United States condemns Kagame's atrocities, while on the other hand, it continues to build the Rwandan military that commits these crimes. While President Obama's 2012 rebuke of Rwanda's violence in DRC led to the suspension of a small portion of military aid, the United States hardly reversed course. American military support to Rwanda increased to its previous levels within a short period.

Chapter 7 looks at Kagame's latest delusion of grandeur—reinforcing the capacity of the African Union. Kagame's qualification is his purported transformation of Rwanda into a highly competitive capitalist market that he terms an "African economic lion." This, of course, is nonsense.

Kagame's capitalism is without capitalists. The most successful businesspeople during the Kagame presidency suffered the same fate as the society at large—violence, exile, and even death. What passes for capitalism in Kagame's Rwanda is cronyism centered on his ruling party's conglomerate, which essentially depends on government contracts.

Chapter 8 concludes the book by reflecting on the politics of violence and genocide that transcend Rwanda's power incumbents. In this sense, Kagame is following the footsteps of his postindependence predecessors. Each head of state clung to power until the very end—using violence and the threat of genocide to sustain power—and was removed from power violently. Similarly, today's incumbent has closed all avenues for a peaceful transfer of power, thereby locking himself in the same trajectory as his predecessors.

I dedicate this work to three Rwandan women—Agathe Uwilingiyimana, Victoire Ingabire Umuhoza, and Diane Shima Rwigara. Uwilingiyimana was Rwanda's prime minister who was killed in the 1994 genocide. Uwilingiyimana stood for social justice. As education minister, she abolished the academic ethnic quota system, thus opening educational opportunities to all Rwandans. Ingabire left her family and career in the Netherlands to compete for the presidency with a vision of Rwanda that caters equitably to its diverse communities. The regime instead imprisoned her. Diane Shima Rwigara dared to launch her presidential campaign by defiantly portraying the incumbent regime a human rights abuser and fearmongering autocratic state. Uwilingiyimana,

Umuhoza, and Rwigara share one thing—they were not intimated by the endemic violence that transcends distinct postindependence Rwandan regimes.

Contextualizing Kagame's
Killing Fields

———

MAJOR GENERAL PAUL KAGAME ACCOMPLISHED what most career soldiers can only dream about. He has an astonishing thirty-eight-year war record in which he fought or led armies of three different countries. In 1980, before he could complete his high school education, Kagame joined the Ugandan rebel fighters. Led by Yoweri Museveni, they captured power and formed a government in 1986. After serving in the new Ugandan military, Kagame led his armed struggle in Rwanda beginning in 1990. Kagame's fighting acumen was especially evident between 1994 and 2000 when he became a military legend with a reputation for the audacity, surprise, tempo, and focus to defeat much bigger armies. In 1994, his rebel fighters defeated the genocidal former Rwandan military, sending the remnants of the collapsed regime across the border into the Democratic Republic of Congo (DRC), with more than one million refugees used as human shields. Kagame achieved even more spectacular victories in 1996 and 1997. He destroyed the power structures of the old Rwandan military that had regrouped in eastern DRC, scattering hundreds of thousands of refugees back to Rwanda and deeper into DRC forests. Kagame proceeded to overthrow the thirty-two-year-old dictatorship of Mobutu Sese Seko and installed Laurent Kabila in power, complete with Rwandan military officers in charge of strategic regions and towns, including Kinshasa, the capital city.

By 1997, Kagame had become the predominant occupying power of DRC, a vast country ninety times larger than Rwanda. When Laurent Kabila sought to exert his independence by replacing Rwandan military officers with Congolese nationals, Kagame immediately invaded DRC again. As the US government explains, "War broke out in August 1998, when Kabila tried to expel Rwandan military forces that had helped him to overthrow Mobutu."[1] In 1999 and 2000, Kagame crushed the armies of his former commander and co-occupier of DRC, Uganda's President Museveni, in three battles to gain control over the provincial capital of Kisangani.

Kagame's 1994–2000 military accomplishments had a dark side. The human cost was astronomical. As a result of these wars, an estimated five million people in DRC alone died from mass murder, starvation, disease, malnutrition,

---

1 US Department of State, "DRC—Country Reports on Human Rights Practices 2000," February 23, 2001, https://www.state.gov/j/drl/rls/hrrpt/2000/af/753.htm.

exhaustion, and mass dislocation.[2] The same intense brutality became a way of life in Rwanda, composed of politically motivated murders, disappearances, massacres, and assassinations of members of the Rwandan diaspora considered to be Kagame's opponents. The obsession with violence was also evident during genocide. Kagame ferociously opposed external intervention that might deny him an outright capture of power, leading to more deaths. By comparison, all other mass murder in Africa combined is no match for the Kagame-associated deaths in Rwanda and DRC. Estimates of late twentieth-century mass killings in Africa include 1.5 million lives destroyed by Mengistu Haile Mariam in Ethiopia;[3] between eighty thousand and three hundred thousand killed by Idi Amin;[4] fifteen thousand people killed by Charles Taylor

2   "Testimony Assistant Secretary Johnnie Carson Bureau of African Affairs US Department of State Before the House Committee on Foreign Affairs Subcommittee on Africa, Global Health and Human Rights 'The Devastating Crisis in Eastern Congo,'" Tuesday, December 11, 2012, http://archives.republicans.foreignaffairs.house.gov/112/HHRG-112-FA16-WState-CarsonJ-20121211.pdf.

3   Centre for Security Studies, "Zimbabwe: Call for Mengistu Extradition," http://www.css.ethz.ch/en/services/digital-library/articles/article.html/52764/pdf.

4   Harriet Anena, "How Many People Did Amin Really Kill?," *Daily Monitor*, September 28, 2012, http://www.monitor.co.ug/SpecialReports/ugandaat50/How-many-people-did-Amin-really-kill-/1370466-1519550-k5ak59/index.html.

of Liberia;[5] and seventy thousand casualties in Sierra Leone at the hands of Foday Sankoh, among others.[6]

From this history, it becomes apparent that Kagame's success was not limited to defeating larger armies and occupying territories. Even more extraordinary was his ability to contain and whitewash the violent aspect of his legacy while marketing himself as a champion for peace, stability, and development for Rwanda and Africa. Kagame cultivated an image that is the opposite of his actual history of violence. In this sense, Kagame was a manipulative genius. He was able to recast himself as a man who not only stopped genocide in Rwanda but also became the leading peacekeeper on the troubled African continent. To this rebranding, Kagame added the claim that he transformed Rwanda from a poor country dependent on subsistence agriculture into a stable, peaceful, democratic, and prosperous African economic lion in a single generation. Based on this purported achievement, fellow African presidents awarded Kagame the responsibility of turning the African Union (AU) into a dynamic, self-financing organization, free from foreign aid dependency.

Kagame's genius was further illustrated by his ability to forestall legal processes that sought to hold him accountable for violence in Rwanda, DRC, and elsewhere. For example, in 2006, Kagame successfully circumvented trial in a case filed by the DRC government at the International Court of Justice (ICJ)

5 Mission in Liberia, "Background," http://www.un.org/en/peacekeeping/missions/unmil/background.shtml.

6 UNDP, Case of Sierra Leone, 2006, http://web.undp.org/evaluation/documents/thematic/conflict/SierraLeone.pdf.

for causing the death of 3.5 million Congolese. Rather than deal with the substance of the case, Kagame cunningly used a legal maneuver to deny the ICJ jurisdiction over Rwanda. In 2010, when the United Nations published the DRC Mapping Exercise Report, documenting more than six hundred cases of atrocities, including possible genocide against Rwandan refugees in DRC, Kagame ridiculed and rejected the report.[7] He then forced the United Nations to shelve the mapping report by threatening to withdraw his peacekeeping troops from African conflict hotspots. The United Nations Secretary-General Ban Ki-moon traveled to Rwanda to plead with Kagame not to remove his troops, including the thirty-five hundred in Darfur, Sudan, led by Rwandan General Patrick Nyamvumba.[8] Kagame won—the mapping report was forgotten. In 2011, the Rwandan president sought and received reprieve from the Obama administration, which filed immunity on his behalf, to avoid a US $350 million lawsuit alleging that Kagame killed his predecessor and his Burundian counterpart, thus triggering the 1994 Rwandan genocide.[9]

---

7   United Nations Human Rights Commission, "Democratic Republic of the Congo Mapping Exercise Report, 1993–2003," http://www.ohchr.org/Documents/Countries/CD/DRC_MAPPING_REPORT_FINAL_EN.pdf.

8   Cecile Aptel, "The UN Mapping Report Documenting Serious Crimes in the Democratic Republic of the Congo," *American Society of International Law* 14, no. 18 (November 17, 2010), https://www.asil.org/insights/volume/14/issue/38/un-mapping-report-documenting-serious-crimes-democratic-republic-congo.

9   In the United States Court of Appeals for the Tenth Circuit, Madame Habyarimana, et al., Plaintiffs-Appellants, v. Paul Kagame, Defendant-Appellee. On Appeal from the United States District Court for the Western District of Oklahoma, https://www.state.gov/documents/organization/211933.pdf.

Kagame's manipulative genius is also evident in his anticipating and nullifying legal traps that lie ahead. The 2015-amended Rwandan constitution exempts Kagame from prosecution when he is no longer head of state. According to Article 114, "A former President of the Republic cannot be prosecuted for treason or serious and deliberate violation of the Constitution when no legal proceedings in respect of that offense were brought against him or her while in office."[10] With Article 114, Kagame has built an impenetrable legal fence to protect himself for life. The article is a license to kill more people that guarantees freedom from justice for life.

---

10   Republic of Rwanda, "The Constitution of the Republic of Rwanda of 2003, Revised in 2015," http://www.parliament.gov.rw/fileadmin/Bills_CD/ THE_CONSTITUTION_OF_THE_REPUBLIC_OF_RWANDA_ OF_2003_REVISED_IN_2015.pdf.

CHAPTER 2

Kagame's Power Hunger and the Rwandan Genocide

——

KAGAME NARRATES THE 1994 RWANDAN genocide in terms of "good guys" versus "bad guys." The bad guys are the United Nations, its member states, and the officials who failed to stop the 1994 Rwandan genocide. The good guys are Kagame and the Rwandan Patriotic Front (RPF), who stopped the genocide. This is Kagame describing the bad guys in April 2017:

> There were long debates, where some countries who want to change history and shift responsibility for their role in what happened in Rwanda onto Rwandans, even those who survived…The United Nations is difficult to define. It is used by countries who blame it when things go wrong and take credit when things go right.[11]

---

11   Remarks by President Paul Kagame Kwibuka 23, Kigali, April 7, 2017,   http://www.paulkagame.com/index.php/speeches/1814-remarks-by-president-paul-kagame-kwibuka-23-kigali-7-april-2017.

Typically, Kagame's views and statements are dismissive of the international community, as in the following: "Forget about the outside world—where so many people have been rightly accused of having stood by when the genocide was happening…Forget about the nonsense of international justice…These are the same people who want to give us lessons every day."[12] Here is Kagame recounting the good guys, composed of himself and the RPF, who liberated Rwanda from its past ills:

> The liberation was about rescuing ourselves from a pre- and post-independence leadership that fostered and promoted hatred, sectarianism and genocidal ideologies—culminating in the decision to exterminate its own citizens. This created a legacy of bad politics, poor governance, disastrous social development philosophies and practices, and an economic system that entrenched a vicious cycle of poverty and dependency. These pre-liberation governments largely ignored the country's most precious resource—its people—through substandard education and health policies and sidelined productive enterprise for a system of cronyism within subsistence agriculture that failed to benefit the ordinary Rwandan. It was these circumstances that inspired us to liberate our country

12 Speech by President Kagame at the 17th Genocide Commemoration Ceremony, Kigali, April 7, 2011, http://www.paulkagame.com/index.php/speeches/314-president-kagame-speech-at-the-17th-commemoration-of-the-genocide-against-the-tutsis-kigali-7th-april-2011.

and begin the journey of building a nation worthy of our people.[13]

Sometimes Kagame includes fellow Africans among the good guys—"Africa, almost all the countries, stood up...I want to thank Africans for this."[14]

Kagame's story of good and bad guys does not stand up to scrutiny, beginning with the definition of the term "genocide." His definition has changed over time, according to political convenience. In the 1990s, Kagame articulated the Rwandan genocide in broader terms. According to him, while members of the Tutsi community were targeted for extermination, other communities were also victims of the violence that swept across Rwanda. For example, on April 8, 1994, two days after genocide started, Kagame stated that the then "Rwandan army is killing officials and Tutsis."[15] Kagame and his RPF continued to frame the genocide in the same broad terms in 1994. For example, castigating the United Nations on April 30, 1994, for restricting the term "genocide" to Tutsi only, the RPF asserted that, "The false impression that this is an ethnic conflict needs to be corrected." The more accurate

---

13 Speech by His Excellency Paul Kagame, president of the Republic of Rwanda, on Liberation Day, Kigali, July 4, 2009, http://www.paulkagame. com/index.php/speeches/85-liberation-day-kigali-4-july-2009.

14 Remarks by President Paul Kagame Kwibuka 23, Kigali, April 7, 2017, http://www.paulkagame.com/index.php/speeches/1814-remarks-by-president-paul-kagame-kwibuka-23-kigali-7-april-2017.

15 The US Department of State, Confidential, "Situation Report as of April 8, 1994," Colonel Parker, Defense Attaché, talking to Major General Paul Kagame, http://nsarchive.gwu.edu/NSAEBB/NSAEBB119/Rw12.pdf.

characterization of what was going on, according to the RPF, would include the tens of thousands of members of the Hutu community who were also killed:

> The massacres are not above all the result of the fighting between two different ethnic groups as the statement of the UN Secretary-General would appear to indicate. Although the Tutsi community has been singled out as a candidate for extermination, Rwandese of other ethnicities have equally been victims of the atrocities. Tens of thousands of Hutus have died because they belonged to opposition parties. Indeed the majority of prominent public personalities who were executed were Hutus.[16]

The US government expressed a similar view, stating that the seven hundred members of the Rwandan presidential guard and their extremist Hutu civilian supporters unleashed a "systematic campaign of murder and genocide," killing "hundreds of Tutsi and Hutu opposition leaders and their families."[17] This broader view is what led to the term "Rwandan genocide," recognizing that the Tutsi community was targeted for

---

16   Rwandan Patriotic Front, "Statement of the Political Bureau of the Rwandan Patriotic Front on the Proposed Deployment of the UN Intervention Force in Rwanda," April 30, 1994, https://www.documentcloud.org/documents/1687041-footnote-12-pt-2-rpf-statement-april-30.html.

17   US Department of State, ""Rwanda—Country Reports on Human Rights Practices, 1994," February 1995, http://dosfan.lib.uic.edu/ERC/democracy/1994_hrp_report/94hrp_report_africa/Rwanda.html.

extermination but also acknowledging that members of the Hutu and Twa communities were massacred.

Later, Kagame made a U-turn. He rebranded genocide as committed exclusively against Tutsi, thereby erasing other communities from the definition. Anyone who deviated from the new and narrower definition became a genocide denier, and therefore a criminal. In October 2014, the BBC aired a documentary film, *Rwanda's Untold Story*, which articulated the broader view of genocide in which not only Tutsi died but also Hutu. Kagame banned the broadcaster's local-language channel. The Kagame government charged the makers of the documentary with hatred, revisionism, and genocide denial. Kagame denounced the British and the BBC for "cynicism of the highest order" in the following language:

> They chose to tarnish Rwandans, to dehumanize them, and deny the very genocide they reported on. This is coming from a part of the world that has a lot of instructions to give us about freedoms. This is not the first time, we see it every day, every week, every month in all forms...The freedom they teach us is different when it comes to Rwanda...I am saying this to remind you that no one owes you a thing, you are on your own and you should own it. You should own your story, own everything about it, shape it the way you want.[18]

---

18   Cited in Edwin Musoni, "Kagame Speaks Out on BBC Genocide Denial," *The New Times*, October 15, 2014, http://www.newtimes.co.rw/section/article/2014-10-15/181977/.

Before the *Rwanda's Untold Story* documentary, the leader of United Democratic Forces, Victoire Ingabire, had expressed the broader view in 2010—a perspective indistinguishable from Kagame's definition in 1994. As she explained, "If we say 'Hutus were also victims,' for the government, this is genocide ideology. There was a genocide, but there were also other crimes in Rwanda, there were crimes against humanity, and we have to remember all the victims of this tragedy."[19] The Rwandan Supreme Court found Ingabire guilty of propagating genocide ideology, sentencing her to fifteen years in 2013. And yet, what Ingabire said was precisely what Kagame himself used to claim.

So what changed? Kagame's political needs and audiences changed. He became a master at modifying the Rwandan genocide to fit different occasions. In 1994, Kagame sought to reassure Rwandans and the international community that he was an inclusive leader, ready to unite and reconcile Rwandans. He wanted to convey the image that he was not an ethnic political operator but a unifier of the Rwandan nation. That is why he used the term "Rwandan genocide," which was inclusive of all Rwandans who had lost their loved ones.

After consolidating power, however, Kagame needed to change his definition for three main reasons. First, he had to intimidate the international community. A restrictive definition of genocide shut the door to any external investigation of Kagame's own atrocities on the Hutu community. Any one international organization seeking to investigate Hutu deaths

---

19 Victoire Ingabire, quoted Nick Wadhams, "Is Rwanda's Hero Becoming Its Oppressor?" *Time*, April 24, 2010, http://content.time.com/time/world/article/0,8599,1984315,00.html.

would be criminalized for advocating double genocide theories. For Kagame and RPF, the correct terminology was "genocide against Tutsi." Second, Kagame had to intimidate Hutu. Any Hutu political leader speaking of Hutu victims during the 1990s would be criminalized. Third, Kagame became the supreme defender of the Tutsi; no other Tutsi could speak for them. The term "genocide against Tutsi" was, therefore, a protective enclosure defending the interests of one man—Kagame.

Kagame gave himself a monopoly over the Rwandan genocide. He alone owns it. That is what he means when he states, "You should own your story, own everything about it, shape it the way you want."[20] And he indeed has done that brilliantly in the past twenty-three years, by owning the story of genocide, and by shaping it the way he wants.

The most shocking aspect about Kagame's role in the 1994 genocide, however, was not his U-turn in defining it. Far from it. The astonishing factor was his refusal to cooperate with the United Nations to deploy an intervention force after the latter realized its initial blunder of not doing enough. We see the RPF ferociously objecting to the UN and even threatening the multilateral body from April 1994 to the very end of genocide, three months later. On April 30, 1994, the RPF "categorically opposed" the United Nations' intervention force in the following terms:

The time for the UN intervention is long past. The genocide is almost completed. Most of the potential

20 Cited in Musoni, "Kagame Speaks Out on BBC Genocide Denial."

victims of the regime have either been killed or fled…Consequently, the Rwandese Patriotic Front hereby declares that it is categorically opposed to the proposed UN intervention force and will not under any circumstances cooperate in its setting and operation…[T]he deployment of the proposed force as UN intervention can no longer serve any useful purpose as far as stopping the massacres is concerned.[21]

Kagame was to repeat these same statements five days later. On this particular occasion, Kagame was addressing the United Nations officials who were attempting to persuade him to accept an expanded intervention force. Kagame would have none of it, stating at the end of the meeting that he was "opposed to what they called intervention force because we felt it was irrelevant in the circumstances." He added that he "did not understand what that intervention would serve as a purpose when genocide has been carried out in this country almost with impunity and when it is near completion people talk about intervention."[22] Imagine that—Kagame was

---

21 Rwandan Patriotic Front, "Statement of the Political Bureau of the Rwandan Patriotic Front on the Proposed Deployment of the UN Intervention Force in Rwanda."

22 Paul Kagame, *Rwanda: Rebel Leader Negotiates with the UN* (New York: Associated Press, May 5, 1994), http://www.aparchive.com/search?startd=& endd=&allFilters=&query=Kagame+rebel+leader+negotiates+with+UN&ad vsearchStartDateFilter=&advsearchEndDateFilter=&searchFilterHdSDFor mat=All&searchFilterDigitized=All&searchFiltercolorFormat=All&searchFi lteraspectratioFormat=All.

making these statements on May 5, 1994, while genocide was spreading around Rwanda.

Kagame's rejection and hostility to the United Nations' intervention in April and May 1994 was most disgraceful for someone who ceaselessly masquerades as the hero who stopped genocide in Rwanda. Imagine a European leader objecting to the United States' entry into the Second World War because the Americans were late in joining the war effort. According to this inexplicable reasoning, the United States' intervention between 1943 and 1945 would have made no difference. This, of course, is most absurd—the belated American intervention was decisive in ending the war and saving lives. A late intervention by the United Nations in Rwandan genocide would have saved lives. Even a single day of saving lives is morally right and materially vital. In the case of Rwanda, Kagame was objecting to external intervention in the very month genocide started.

In April 1994, at the time Kagame was objecting to the United Nations' intervention, even the RPF was citing a figure of five hundred thousand killed. In its statement of April 30, 1994, RPF asserted that as a result of the massacres, "a half million people (500,000) may have already died."[23] One would, therefore, have expected the RPF to welcome the new intervention force, as well as for Kagame to be frantically demanding a more forceful military support and not shutting the door on intervention. We will, of course, never know

---

23   RPF to the UN Security Council, April 30, 1994, https://www.documentcloud.org/documents/1687041-footnote-12-pt-2-rpf-statement-april-30.html.

how many Rwandans might have been saved had Kagame adopted a more collaborative mindset. Kagame had different concerns at this point. As the international community discussed a more robust and better-mandated force to protect Rwandans, Kagame was preoccupied with the acquisition of absolute power. His biggest fear was that somehow external forces would deny him total victory and the future presidency of Rwanda. He wanted absolute power and on his terms. Lives did not matter. Kagame also worried that international intervention forces would have witnessed his atrocities. As we see in chapter 3, this is what happened at Kibeho a year later, when Kagame's military massacred thousands of Rwandans in the presence of the United Nations intervention forces.

Kagame was not yet done opposing external intervention. He now became obsessed with the size of the intervention force, demanding that the number of troops should not be more than the original force deployed before genocide. Here is the RPF's position as of May 12, 1994, regarding the number of troops: "The proposed force is far in excess of what is necessary to protect civilians in danger and facilitate the distribution of humanitarian assistance...The Rwandan Patriotic Front recommends a UN force of the size of the original [United Nations Assistance Mission for Rwanda] UNAMIR (2,500)."[24] On May 16, 1994, RPF reminded the United Nations: "As we have stated before, it is the view of the Rwandese Patriotic Front that a force the size of 5,500 is

24 Rwandan Patriotic Front, "Consultation on Deployment of the Proposed UN Force in Rwanda," May 12, 1994, https://www.documentcloud.org/documents/1392945-footnote-148-rpf-may-12-statement.html.

too large and unacceptable for the envisaged mission."[25] And on June 21, 1994, RPF issued the following veiled threat to the United Nations:

> The Rwandese Patriotic Front is concerned that its personnel may not always be in position to make a clear distinction between UNAMIR and other foreign forces in the event of escalation of hostilities. We have, regrettably, come to the conclusion that it is necessary that UNAMIR be withdrawn.[26]

Years after he had left office, Bill Clinton, who was the American president during the 1994 Rwandan genocide, estimated that had he provided ten thousand troops, more than three hundred thousand Rwandan lives could have been saved.[27] But here was Kagame demanding total withdrawal of the United Nations forces—in the middle of a genocide. What we learn from Kagame's views and role in the genocide is how little we know about this period of Rwandan history. Nonetheless, as the old Rwandan regime crumbled after executing genocide, the new elite was working hard to take power at any cost.

---

25 Rwandan Patriotic Front, "Rwandese Patriotic Front Statement to the UN Security Council," May 16, 1994, http://rwandafile.com/table/pdf/rpf0516.pdf.

26 Rwandese Patriotic Front, June 21, 1994, http://rwandafile.com/table/pdf/nz2826.pdf.

27 Jake Flanagin, "Bill Clinton Failed to Stop Genocide in Rwanda, but His Foundation Is Quietly Making Amends," April 16, 2015, https://qz.com/384228/the-clinton-foundation-is-atoning-for-bills-failure-on-rwanda/.

In hindsight, we observe that there were hardly any "good guys" in the Rwandan genocide, least of all the two men who later became protector and beneficiary—Bill Clinton and Paul Kagame. The United Nations' inability to do more in preventing genocide in Rwanda was primarily the work of President Clinton and his government. One declassified memo from the US National Security Council sums up the Clinton administration's attitude: "Rwanda may be the case the NSC is looking for to prove that the US can say no to a new peacekeeping operation. Given the lack of enthusiasm in the rest of government for the Rwanda operation...we may have to say no with a veto."[28] We know what followed this apathy—death of up to one million people. These Rwandans were predominantly Tutsi, targeted for slaughter as a group. But included in these deaths were members of Hutu and Twa populations. As Kagame and RPF had rightly stated in 1994, although members of the Tutsi community were singled out for extermination, Rwandese of other ethnicities were also victims.

Clinton's role in the Rwandan genocide deserves a few more comments. Here was a head of state who, by self-admission, watched the Rwandan genocide unfold but actively prevented his government and the United Nations from intervening. To compensate for his guilt, Clinton built Kagame's army while still in office. Then Clinton romanticized Kagame by including him in the infamous "new breed

---

28   Dick Clark, Senior Member, the National Security Council, "The NSC Is Downbeat on a Rwanda Operation," http://nsarchive.gwu.edu/NSAEBB/NSAEBB511/docs/DOCUMENT%202.pdf.

of African leaders" supposedly committed to democracy, the rule of law, and good governance. Once out of office, Clinton became an even bolder Kagame champion. Here is Clinton's description of Kagame when granting him a global citizenship award in 2009:

> His Excellency Paul Kagame, President of the Republic of Rwanda, has led his nation through an unparalleled transformation. A brilliant military commander, President Kagame joined Rwanda's transitional government after leading the force which ended the 1994 genocide…President Kagame's national leadership has proven to be as bold as his military campaigns: creating visionary policies, innovative national programs, and strong international partnerships to support the development of the new Rwanda. President Kagame has worked to develop infrastructure, boost tourism, increase access to energy and health care in rural areas, expand exports, and develop ties to the international business community…From crisis, President Kagame has forged a strong, unified and growing nation with the potential to become a model for the rest of Africa and the world.[29]

---

29 "President Clinton Announces Winners of Global Citizenship Awards," September 23, 2009, http://www.prnewswire.com/news-releases/president-clinton-announces-winners-of-the-third-annual-clinton-global-citizen-awards-60762922.html.

By now, Rwanda had become the centerpiece of the Clinton Foundation's philanthropic endeavors, which were invested heavily in agribusinesses and health. Meanwhile, Tony Blair in Britain was also building and flattering Kagame's brand. According to Blair, it is through Kagame's "visionary leadership that Rwanda has become the African success story it is today, a country moving in the right direction at a remarkable pace."[30] Not all was perfect with Kagame and Clinton, as we learned from the leaked e-mails in 2016. Clinton Foundation officials were worried about "reputational issues," especially how William J. Clinton's name was being used, "given the sensitivity of WJC's relationship with Kagame."[31] This does not sound like a vote of confidence for the Rwandan president.

Besides Kagame sacrificing fellow Rwandans for power, the main lesson from the Rwandan genocide is how he became a master of scapegoating the international community. In the United Nations, Kagame finds a perfect target for bullying and scapegoating. He might still identify myriad other possibilities for intimidating the multilateral agency while benefitting politically, especially since he became a leading supplier to the United Nations' peacekeeping operations. Little wonder that the United Nations Secretary-General Ban

---

30 "Tony Blair Meets with 'Visionary Leader' Paul Kagame During Latest Two-Day Visit to Rwanda," November 16, 2009, http://www.tonyblairoffice. org/news/entry/tony-blair-meets-with-visionary-leader-paul-kagame-during-latest-two-day-vi/.

31 From:zshaikley@clintonfoundation.org To: blindsey@clintonfoundation.org, adesai@clintonfoundation.org CC: wmorris@clintonfoundation.org, john.podesta@gmail.com Date: 2012-01-06 21:24 Subject: RE: CHDI? https://wikileaks.org/podesta-emails/emailid/21889.

Ki-moon even credited Kagame for bringing democracy and human rights to Rwanda. Here is Ban Ki-moon is his own words:

> I highly commend the leadership of President Paul Kagame who led this country [from] such a tragic genocide in just 20 years, made shining examples of socioeconomic development and also of democracy, protecting and preserving human rights of all the people. I hope that these shining examples will be emulated by many other countries. We have to learn the lessons...We have President Paul Kagame as one of the great African leaders who have been contributing greatly to the peace and stability...We will continue to work for peace and stability and development.[32]

---

32   Ban Ki-moon, "Remarks of the Secretary-General Ban Ki-moon, Following His Meeting with Rwanda's President Paul Kagame," April 6, 2014, https://www.un.org/sg/en/content/sg/press-encounter/2014-04-06/remarks-secretary-general-following-his-meeting-rwandas.

CHAPTER 3

Kagame's Killing Fields in Rwanda

———

KAGAME COULD NOT HAVE POSSIBLY launched his killing fields in Rwanda more dramatically. In June 1994, his army killed thirteen clergymen at Kabwayi in central Rwanda, including the archbishop of Kigali, Vincent Nsengiyumva; the Bishop of Byumba, Joseph Ruzindana; and the Bishop of Kabgayi, Thadee Nsengiyumya, who was also then president of the Conference of Catholic Bishops of Rwanda.[33] The following year witnessed an even more catastrophic episode. It happened at the Kibeho camp for internally displaced persons, holding between eighty thousand and one hundred thousand people. More than four thousand Rwandans were massacred in the presence of, among others, the Australian contingent of the United Nations intervention force. An Australian government document describes what happened:

---

[33] US Department of State, "Rwanda—Country Reports on Human Rights Practices, 1994, February 1995, http://dosfan.lib.uic.edu/ERC/democracy/1994_hrp_report/94hrp_report_africa/Rwanda.html.

On 19 April 1995, a group of 32 Australian soldiers and medical personnel were sent to the Kibeho refugee camp to assist refugees and UNAMIR activities. The situation within the camp was desperate... From 20 to 23 April the RPF began to close down and empty the camp. The already tense situation descended into a violent massacre, with the RPF killing around 4,000 people and injuring 600. The medical team, led by Captain Carol Vaughan-Evans, struggled to cope with the sheer volume of wounded... Under UNAMIR's mandate, the troops and peacekeepers could have intervened in the conflict but were seriously outnumbered by RPF and risked also being killed. Moreover, it would have been hard to fire without killing refugees. Hence, under the command of Lieutenant Steve Tilbrook, the Australian infantrymen did not open fire to defend the refugees—a situation the men found particularly distressing. A debriefing team was later sent to Rwanda to counsel the Australians who were present at the massacre. It was later argued that UN presence at Kibeho stopped the RPF from killing everyone in the camp and creating an even worse outcome.[34]

To get a sense of Kagame's killing fields since the Kibeho massacre, I have compiled names, dates, and locations of

---

34 Australian War Memorial, "Rwanda (UNAMIR) 1993–1996," https:// www.awm.gov.au/unit/U60680/.

deaths from the US Department of State's annual reports from 1994 to 2016. This history is summarized, after which I show the Rwandan official explanations of these killings, including Kagame's own views. The summaries are presented in chronological order and placed in three categories, namely, "targeted killings," "disappearances," and "massacres."

Targeted Killings, Disappearances, and Massacres by the Rwandan Patriotic Army (RPA)/Rwanda Defense Forces (RDF) and the Rwanda National Police (RNP), 1994–2016

1994   Targeted killing: "In June, 3 RPA soldiers murdered 13 Hutu priests, including the Archbishop of Kigali, in Kabgayi."[35]

1995   Massacre: "In March near Bugarama an RPA unit summarily executed 17 civilians after being ambushed by suspected Hutu militiamen."

       Massacre: "On September 11, members of the RPA killed more than 110 civilians in Kanama after an ambush of an RPA vehicle. The Government admitted that this was the result of excessive force, and has investigated, but has produced no results by year's end."

---

35 US Department of State, "Rwanda—Country Reports on Human Rights Practices, 1994, February 1995, http://dosfan.lib.uic.edu/ERC/democracy/1994_hrp_report/94hrp_report_africa/Rwanda.html.

<u>Massacre</u>: "In April the military fired into a panicked crowd at the internally displaced persons camp at Kibeho, killing hundreds."[36]

1996   <u>Disappearance</u>: "[T]here were a growing number of incommunicado detentions by agents of the State, which resulted in the effective disappearance of many persons."

<u>Massacre</u>: "The RPA committed hundreds of killings for political reasons, in revenge for earlier violence, and in security sweeps...The RPA killed many civilians during these operations." [37]

1997   <u>Targeted killing</u>: "On January 16, Evaniste Burakali, an outspoken member of the National Assembly and the Liberal Party was killed."

<u>Targeted killing</u>: "On October 4, Jean-Baptiste Safari, known to be a sympathizer of the exile opposition group was killed outside his home."

<u>Massacre</u>: "From January through August, the RPA may have killed as many as 6,000 persons. The RPA admits to civilian killings, but says that its troops cannot distinguish between insurgents wearing civilian clothing and innocent bystanders." [38]

---

36   US Department of State, "Rwanda—Country Reports on Human Rights Practices, 1995, March 1996, http://dosfan.lib.uic.edu/ERC/democracy/1995_hrp_report/95hrp_report_africa/Rwanda.html.

37   US Department of State, "Rwanda—Country Reports on Human Rights Practices 1996, 1997, http://www.refworld.org/docid/3ae6aa2316.html.

38   US Department of State, "Rwanda—Country Reports on Human Rights Practices 1997, January 1998, https://www.state.gov/www/global/

Massacre: "After we located between 80,000 and 100,000 refugees south of Kisangani [at Tingi Tingi], urgent life-saving assistance was given...For four days access to the camp was banned. When we were allowed to return, we found only abandoned huts, but no refugees...I am disturbed about the apparently organized and systematic attacks on refugees."[39] Of nearly one million refugees and internally displaced people in Zaire, 220,000 refugees were "unaccounted for."[40]

1998 Targeted killing: May 16, 1998, Seth Sendashonga was killed in Nairobi, Kenya. "A police investigation into the shooting to death of former Rwandan Minister Seth Sendashonga was ongoing at year's end."[41]

Massacre: "The RPA committed hundreds of extrajudicial killings, including individuals and families, in the course of fighting the insurgency in the northwest. The RPA generally committed these abuses during security sweeps, and in revenge for earlier killings

---

human_rights/1997_hrp_report/rwanda.html.

39 Remarks by Mrs. Sadako Ogata, United Nations High Commissioner for Refugees, at the United Nations Security Council, New York, April 28, 1997, http://www.unhcr.org/admin/hcspeeches/3ae68fbb1c/remarks-mrs-sadako-ogata-united-nations-high-commissioner-refugees-united.html.

40 Lords Hansard, statement by Baroness Chalker of Wallasey, https://www.publications.parliament.uk/pa/ld199697/ldhansrd/vo970227/text/70227w02.htm.

41 U.S. Department of State, "Kenya—Country Reports on Human Rights Practices 1998, 1999, https://www.justice.gov/sites/default/files/eoir/legacy/2013/06/07/hrp98kenya.pdf

by insurgent militias. Victims of RPA operations included elderly persons, women, and children…"[42]

1999 Disappearance: Persons arrested and detained in DRC "were transferred to Rwanda and remained unaccounted for at year's end."

Massacre: "Since the start of the current war in the DRC in August 1998, RPA troops have participated on the side of the Congolese rebel movement Rassemblement Congolais pour la Democratie (RCD) against the DRC Government. There have been many reports, some of which were credible, that RPA soldiers massacred civilians in the DRC."[43]

2000 Targeted killing: "On March 5, three men reportedly in military uniform shot and killed Assiel Kabera, an advisor to then-President Bizimungu, outside his house…No one was arrested or charged in Kabera's murder by year's end."[44]

2001 Targeted killing: "In February in Kigali, a soldier in uniform killed RPA officer Alphonse Mbayire, a former military attaché assigned to the Rwandan Embassy in Nairobi…there were unconfirmed reports of government involvement in the killing because

42 US Department of State, "Rwanda—Country Reports on Human Rights Practices, 1998, https://www.state.gov/j/drl/rls/hrrpt/1999/266.htm.

43 US State Department, "Rwanda—Country Reports on Human Rights Practices, 1999," February 2000, https://www.state.gov/j/drl/rls/hrrpt/1999/266.htm.

44 US State Department, "Rwanda—Country Reports on Human Rights Practices, 2000," February 2001, https://www.state.gov/j/drl/rls/hrrpt/2000/af/720.htm.

of information Mbayire may have had concerning the 1998 murder in Nairobi of former Minister of Internal Affairs Seth Sendashonga. No action reportedly was taken against the soldier by year's end."

<u>Disappearance</u>: "[S]everal persons disappeared, including RPA members. Most persons who were reported missing reappeared in other countries, claiming that they were forced to flee for their own safety; however, some remained missing and were presumed dead at year's end…"

<u>Disappearance</u>: "On April 27, Theobald Rwaka Gakwaya, the founder of the Rwandan League for the Promotion and Defense of Human Rights who lost his position as Interior Minister in March after numerous disagreements with the Government, disappeared…There were unconfirmed reports at year's end that Gakwaya was in self-imposed exile."

<u>Massacre</u>: "RPA Captain Peter Kabanda and other RPA soldiers who allegedly killed 67 unarmed civilians in Masisi, North Kivu Province, DRC, in 2000, remained in detention…"

<u>Massacre</u>: "No action reportedly was taken against the RPA officers responsible for human rights violations in 2000 during fighting with Ugandan army troops in Kisangani, which resulted in hundreds of civilian deaths, more than 1,700 persons injured, and 60,000 displaced persons."[45]

---

45 US State Department, "Rwanda—Country Reports on Human Rights Practices, 2001," March 2002, https://www.state.gov/j/drl/rls/hrrpt/2001/af/8398.htm.

2002 Massacre: "The reported extrajudicial killings of civilians by RCD and Rwandan forces in the DRC often reportedly were committed in reprisal for guerrilla attacks on RCD or RDF forces...There were numerous credible reports that RDF and RCD/Goma troops burned and destroyed entire villages in the DRC, frequently killing, torturing, or raping some of the inhabitants, especially in rural areas of North and South Kivu and northern Maniema Province. In May RCD-Goma troops killed more than 100 persons in retaliation for an attempted mutiny by RCD-Goma dissidents in Kisangani, DRC."[46]

2003 Targeted killing: "On March 7, two members of the LDF shot and killed Valens Nzigiyimana, Vice Mayor in Charge of Social Affairs in Gitarama Province. On July 18, a LDF officer killed a man named Saidi in Gisenyi Province. On August 31, Protogene Maniragaba, an LDF officer, killed Isidore Ndaraye in Ruhengeri Province; the LDF officer also injured Straton Mbarushimana."

Disappearance: "On April 7, MDR parliamentarian Dr. Leonard Hitimana disappeared in Kigali City. Hitimana was 1 of 48 individuals named in the government report on the MDR..."

Disappearance: "On April 23, Lieutenant-Colonel Augustin Cyiza and Eliezar Runyaruka, a magistrate

---

46   US State Department, "Rwanda—Country Reports on Human Rights Practices, 2002," March 2003, https://www.state.gov/j/drl/rls/hrrpt/2002/18221.htm.

at Nyamata district court, disappeared in Kigali City on their way from UNILAK University. Their vehicle was found at Bukamba district, Ruhengeri province, bordering Uganda, and neither has been heard from since." [47]

2004 Disappearance: "On October 6, police arrested four campaign workers of former Prime Minister Faustin Twagiramungu, who ran in the 2003 presidential elections. The families of Jean de Dieu Kwizera, David Habimana, Block Mugambira, and Jean Paul Kamondo last heard from the four men on October 21, and by year's end, had been given no news of their whereabouts...

Disappearance: On November 20, an RDF captain, Jean Leanard Kagabo, disappeared after police arrested him in Byumba Province. By year's end, his family had been given no news of his whereabouts." [48]

2006 Targeted killing: "On November 24, police officers took into custody and subsequently killed three men—Jean Hakizamungu, John Rukundo, and Francois Ndagijimana—who were suspects in the November 23 killing of Egide Ndabakuranye, the

47   US State Department, "Rwanda—Country Reports on Human Rights Practices, 2003," February 2004, https://www.state.gov/j/drl/rls/hrrpt/2003/27744.htm.

48   US State Department, "Rwanda—Country Reports on Human Rights Practices, 2004," February 2005, https://www.state.gov/j/drl/rls/hrrpt/2004/41621.htm.

president of one of the local jurisdictions comprising a community-based justice system (gacaca)."

Disappearance: "There were no developments in the 2003 disappearances of two prominent citizens and four high-level government officials, including former supreme court vice-president Lieutenant Colonel Cyiza and former parliamentarian Leonard Hitimana, a member of the Democratic Republican Movement (MDR)...Unlike in the previous year, there were no reports that the family and friends who have been supporting the children of Hitimana were harassed." [49]

2010 Targeted killing: "There were two high-profile killings, that of a vice president of an unregistered opposition party and an independent journalist..."[50] On June 24, 2010, Jean-Léonard Rugambage, a Rwandan journalist and acting editor of the newspaper Umuvugizi, was shot dead in Kigali, Rwanda.

Targeted killing: On July 14, 2010, the body of André Kagwa Rwisereka, vice-chairman of the Democratic Green Party, was found partially beheaded near Butare, Rwanda.

---

49   US State Department, "Rwanda—Country Reports on Human Rights Practices, 2006," February 2007, https://www.state.gov/j/drl/rls/hrrpt/2006/81364.htm.

50   US State Department, "Rwanda—Country Reports on Human Rights Practices, 2010," February 2011 https://www.state.gov/documents/organization/160139.pdf.

2011 <u>Targeted killing</u>: "There were several reports that the government attempted to commit arbitrary or unlawful killings within the country and abroad... For example, United Kingdom police in May warned specific Rwandan exiles in London that they were the targets of an assassination plot by the Rwandan government. In June 2010 in Johannesburg, South Africa, an unknown assailant shot and seriously wounded former army chief of staff Faustin Kayumba Nyamwasa..."

<u>Targeted killing</u>: "On September 22, the media reported that South African authorities had foiled another assassination attempt against Kayumba Nyamwasa...On December 1, an unidentified gunman killed Charles Ingabire, a Rwandan journalist, and government critic, in Kampala, Uganda. Both the press and human rights organizations reported that Ingabire had survived an earlier attack in September..."

<u>Targeted killing</u>: "On December 26, an unknown assailant killed FDU-Inkingi member Jerome Ndagijimana in Kampala."

<u>Disappearance</u>: "Rwandan members of a local non-governmental organization (NGO) disappeared along with approximately 80 other people in Rusizi...

Some of those who disappeared...[but] many of the 80 abducted remained missing."[51]

2012 Targeted killing: "On October 15, Mozambique police found former Rwandan Development Board Managing Director Theogene Turatsinze floating dead and tied with ropes in a lake two days after he was reported missing...Domestic political observers commented that Turatsinze had access to politically sensitive financial information related to certain Rwandan government insiders. The killing remained unsolved..."[52]

2013 Targeted killing: "On July 17, Transparency International Rwanda office coordinator Gustave Makonene was strangled to death and his body dumped on the shores of Lake Kivu near the town of Rubavu...Makonene was investigating cases of local police corruption at the time of his death."

Targeted killing: "During the night of December 31, former Rwandan intelligence chief Patrick Karegeya was killed in a hotel room in Johannesburg, South Africa. Karegeya received political asylum in South

51   US State Department, "Rwanda—Country Reports on Human Rights Practices, 2011," 2012, https://www.state.gov/documents/organization/186443.pdf.

52   US State Department, "Rwanda—Country Reports on Human Rights Practices, 2012," 2013, https://www.state.gov/documents/organization/204366.pdf.

Africa in 2009 and resided in the country at the time of his death." [53]

2014 <u>Targeted killing</u>: "On May 17, Alfred Nsengimana, the former executive secretary of Cyuve Sector in Musanze District, was shot and killed while in police custody. Nsengimana was among at least 77 people arrested in Musanze and Rubavu districts from January through May…"

<u>Disappearance</u>: "On June 27, the organizing secretary for the Democratic Green Party of Rwanda (DGPR), Jean Damascene Munyeshyaka, disappeared after meeting with an unknown individual in Nyamata town, Bugesera District."

<u>Disappearance</u>: "The whereabouts of at least 150 individuals reported missing during the March to September security operation remained unknown."

<u>Disappearance</u>: "On June 5, President Kagame defended the government's policy and practices with regard to individuals suspected of posing a threat to state security. During a speech in Nyabihu District, Kagame stated, "those who talk about disappearances…we will continue to arrest more suspects and if possible shoot in broad daylight…"

<u>Massacre</u>: "From July to October, a number of corpses appeared in Lake Rweru, which is bisected by the border between Rwanda and Burundi. Fishermen

---

53 The US Department of State, "Rwanda—Country Reports on Human Rights Practices 2013," 2014, https://www.state.gov/documents/organization/220359.pdf.

reported seeing dozens of floating bodies, some bound and wrapped in sacks…Fishermen living near Kwidagaza reported that on the nights of September 21 and 22, Rwandan marines attempted to exhume the bodies."[54]

2015   Targeted killing: "On February 25, Rwanda National Police (RNP) shot and killed Dr. Emmanuel Gasakure—the personal physician to the president—while he was in custody at the Remera Police Station."

Targeted killing: "Following claims by the family of businessman Assinapol Rwigara that SSF killed Rwigara after a February 4 automobile accident, the City of Kigali seized real estate and in September demolished a hotel belonging to the Rwigara family. The City of Kigali claimed that the hotel had been built without proper permits and was structurally unsound; the family disputed the claim and provided copies of building permits to the press. The family claimed that the government and City of Kigali did not provide compensation for the loss of property and investment."

Disappearance: "On March 26, Illuminee Iragena, a member of the unregistered United Democratic Forces (FDU)-Inkingi party, disappeared…The

---

54 The US Department of State, "Rwanda—Country Reports on Human Rights Practices 2014," 2015, https://www.state.gov/documents/organization/236606.pdf.

government had not initiated an investigation into her disappearance by year's end…"

<u>Disappearance</u>: "[P]olice opened missing persons investigations for all individuals reported missing by families or human rights organizations in 2014, including persons who reportedly disappeared during a March to September 2014 security operation in Musanze and Rubavu conducted by the Rwanda Defense Force (RDF) and the RNP…Of those reported to police, the whereabouts of at least 150 persons remained unknown."[55]

2016 <u>Targeted killing</u>: "On January 23, the Rwanda National Police (RNP) shot and killed Muslim Imam Mohamed Mugemangango while he was in custody…On August 19, RNP officers shot and killed three other Muslim community members in Bugarama…This incident came two days after the RNP in Kigali shot and killed another Muslim, Channy Mbonigaba."

<u>Disappearance</u>: "On March 26, Illuminee Iragena, a member of the unregistered United Democratic Forces (FDU)-Inkingi party, disappeared…"

<u>Disappearance</u>: "On August 7, journalist John Ndabarasa disappeared. Ndabarasa is the brother-in-law of Joel Mutabazi, a former bodyguard to the president, who was convicted…after being deported

55   The US Department of State, "Rwanda—Country Reports on Human Rights Practices 2015," April 2016, https://www.state.gov/j/drl/rls/hrrpt/2015/af/252717.htm.

from Uganda, a move condemned by the UN High Commissioner for Refugees (UNHCR), HRW, and Amnesty International as a violation of the principle of nonrefoulement."

Disappearance: "[T]he organizing secretary for DGPR, Jean Damascene Munyeshyaka, disappeared after meeting with an unknown individual in the town of Nyamata, Bugesera District."[56]

---

56 The US Department of State, "Rwanda—Country Reports on Human Rights Practices 2016," April 2017 https://www.state.gov/j/drl/rls/hrrpt/humanrightsreport/index.htm#wrapper.

As is evident in the above summaries, the period from 2007 and 2009 is not included. This is because no killings appeared in the US Department of State's annual reports. I should also highlight the fact that I am aware of many more Rwandans who were killed or "disappeared" but have omitted them because of the methodology used in this work—only names appearing in official documents are included.

Another government that monitors and reports killings in Rwanda is the United Kingdom. In its case study of March 2015, UK Foreign and Commonwealth Office concluded:

> In January, former Head of Rwandan Intelligence, Patrick Karegeya, was found murdered in a hotel room in Johannesburg, South Africa. In August, a South African court found four men guilty of the attempted assassination of former Rwandan Army Chief of Staff, Kayumba Nyamwasa. The judge concluded that the crime had been "politically motivated" and had "emanated from a certain group of people from Rwanda." The UK is deeply concerned by what appears to be a succession of acts of violence against Rwandan opposition figures.[57]

The UK's case study of Rwanda also indicated that "dozens of local people in northwest Rwanda were arrested and held

---

57   UK Foreign and Commonwealth Office, "Case Study Rwanda—Freedom of Association and Expression," March 15, 2015, https://www.gov.uk/government/case-studies/rwanda-freedom-of-association-and-expression.

incommunicado" and that the UK "regrets that due legal process was not followed."[58]

So, how does the Rwanda government explain these killings, disappearances, and massacres? A good example is the statement by the Rwandan minister of Justice Johnston Busingye. Appearing at the United Nations Commission on Human Rights (UNCHR) on March 18, 2016, the minister was asked to respond to:

> …reported cases of summary or arbitrary execution or enforced disappearance, including the disappearances of political figures such as Augustin Cyiza, Léonard Hitimana, and Jean-Damascene Munyeshyaka, and the executions of André Kagwa Rwisereka and Denis Ntare Semadwinga. The delegation was also asked to comment on reports of assassinations and attempted assassinations of political dissidents abroad, such as the killing of Patrick Karegeya and the attempted killing of Kayumba Nyamwasa in South Africa, and the killing of Charles Ingabire in Uganda…Had such allegations been investigated, and if so, had the persons responsible been brought to justice?[59]

---

58 Ibid.

59 The United Nations Human Rights Office of the Commissioner, "Human Rights Committee Reviews the Report of Rwanda," March 18, 2016, http://www.ohchr.org/EN/NewsEvents/Pages/DisplayNews.aspx?NewsID=18473&LangID=E#sthash.MBjRSrxs.dpuf.

Minister Busingye's response was that "the specific cases of disappearances mentioned...were also of concern to the Government" and that "the Government was working on resolving them."[60]

From the listed deaths in our summaries above, violent deaths have been perpetrated on the Rwandan population every year between 1994 and 2016, except for 2007–2009. That is twenty years of violence. There is hardly any category of Rwandans who has not been subjected to violence. Kagame is not apologetic for this state of being. Responding to criticisms about the never-ending disappearance of Rwandans, Kagame promised, even more, violence: "Those who talk about disappearances...we will continue to arrest more suspects and if possible shoot in broad daylight."[61] Kagame delights in his violence. Reacting to Karegaya's death, for example, the head of state assured his audience that it is a matter of how and when he will eliminate other opponents:

> I was seeing some of our people defending themselves saying: "It wasn't us, we didn't do it" denying the accusations...but my question is: shouldn't we have done it? I really don't feel the necessity for politeness on this issue, no need for being diplomatic, of being politically correct...Because no one will do it for you, no Bangladeshi peacekeeper, no Pakistani, no

---

60   Ibid.

61   The US Department of State, ""Rwanda—Country Reports on Human Rights Practices 2014," 2015, https://www.state.gov/documents/organization/236606.pdf.

white person...Only you can do it, and you shouldn't feel bad about doing what you need to. So I want to tell you, sincerely..., betraying a country, wishing evil upon people has consequences for you. What remains is the how. There are many ways this can happen...Why be ashamed? No one should be ashamed. If it means confrontation using words, then confront each other, if it means confronting using other means, then do that. For me, I signed up even for confrontation.[62]

Kagame, who is an atheist, was gloating in the assassination of his former friend and comrade-in-arms, Patrick Karegeya, at the annual National Prayer Breakfast in Kigali, which brings together Rwandan and international Christian leaders. Nothing can demonstrate Kagame's addiction to violence better than this single event. And the Christians gathered at this event applauded Kagame—possibly more out of fear than appreciation.

---

62 Paul Kagame, "President Paul Kagame's Speech at Rwanda Leaders Fellowship Prayer Breakfast," January 14, 2014, http://www.paulkagame. com/index.php/speeches/1272-president-kagames-speech-at-rwanda-leaders-fellowship-prayer-breakfast.

CHAPTER 4

Kagame's Killing Fields in DRC

———

SPEAKING IN THE BRITISH PARLIAMENT in February 1997, Baroness Lynda Chalker, Minister of State for Overseas Development and Africa at the Foreign Office, summed up the terrible situation facing nearly one million refugees and the internally displaced people in Congo. The refugees were especially in serious danger—two hundred and twenty thousands were "unaccounted for."[63] The sudden disappearance of such a large number of refugees was soon explained by the United Nations High Commissioner for Refugees, Mrs. Sadako Ogata, in her address to the United Nations Security Council in New York on April 28, 1997. Part of Ogata's heartbreaking explanation of the tragic fate of the "unaccounted for" refugees went like this:

> We do not yet know how many lives have been lost through exhaustion, war or outright killing. In

---

63 Lords Hansard, statement by Baroness Chalker of Wallasey, https://www.publications.parliament.uk/pa/ld199697/ldhansrd/vo970227/text/70227w02.htm.

addition, an unknown number of Zairians have been displaced by the conflict. After we located between 80,000 and 100,000 refugees south of Kisangani, urgent life-saving assistance was given and we succeeded in significantly lowering the mortality rate. Our efforts to repatriate the most vulnerable persons by air were repeatedly obstructed. Once again, the refugees were forced to flee following attacks on the camps... For four days access to the camp was banned. When we were allowed to return, we found only abandoned huts, but no refugees...My Office has previously approached the Alliance about alleged human rights abuses. I repeatedly appealed against armed attacks on refugees since the beginning of the offensive, particularly after I visited Tingi Tingi camp in February. I am disturbed about the apparently organized and systematic attacks on refugees.[64]

The 2010 United Nations Human Rights Commission's DRC Mapping Report described these massacres as follows: "In April 1997, when between 60 and 120 refugees were dying each day from disease or exhaustion, AFDL/APR soldiers barred aid agencies and humanitarian NGOs from accessing the camps...On 19 April and 20 April, MSF negotiated entry but was only able to work in the camps for two hours

---

64 Remarks by Mrs. Sadako Ogata, United Nations High Commissioner for Refugees, at the United Nations Security Council, New York, April 28, 1997, http://www.unhcr.org/admin/hcspeeches/3ae68fbb1c/remarks-mrs-sadako-ogata-united-nations-high-commissioner-refugees-united.html.

each day. From 21 April onwards, aid workers were banned entirely from accessing the camps."[65]

What Chalker, Ogata and the UN Congo mapping exercise report were describing was full-scale assaults on refugee camps in Congo, including the catastrophic attack on Tingi Tingi camp that scattered those not yet dead into westward flight yet again. Hundreds of thousands of Rwandan refugees had walked for months from Goma at the border with Rwanda, some 511 km to the east, losing people to disease and exhaustion as they went until they reached Tingi Tingi. They were then massacred, the remaining ones fleeing further west, as Ogata explained. When the United Nations High Commission for Refugees arrived at the scene, they found only "abandoned huts and no refugees."

Six years after the Tingi Tingi massacre, the government of the Democratic Republic of Congo took Rwanda and Uganda to the International Court of Justice (ICJ) for such deaths, including those of Congolese nationals, putting the total number of people killed at 3.5 million. The ICJ, which acts as a world court, decides legal disputes submitted by states.[66] Rwanda and Uganda reacted differently to DRC's charges of crimes against humanity. Rather than argue its case, the Kagame government used Article IX of the United

65 UN Human Rights Commission, DRC Mapping Exercise Report, http://www.ohchr.org/Documents/Countries/CD/DRC_MAPPING_REPORT_FINAL_EN.pdf

66 International Court of Justice, "Jurisdiction," http://www.icj-cij.org/jurisdiction/index.php?p1=5.

Nations' convention on genocide to deny ICJ jurisdiction powers. Article IX reads:

> Disputes between the Contracting Parties relating to the interpretation, application or fulfilment of the present Convention, including those relating to the responsibility of a State for genocide or for any of the other acts enumerated in article III, shall be submitted to the International Court of Justice at the request of any of the parties to the dispute.[67]

Although Rwanda has been a signatory of the genocide convention since April 16, 1975, the then-military dictator Juvenal Habyarimana inserted the following condition: "The Rwandese Republic does not consider itself as bound by Article IX of the convention."[68]

This reservation by Rwanda's old regime proved to be a stroke of luck for Kagame. The reservation effectively nullified the ICJ's jurisdiction over Rwanda. Kagame could therefore legally refuse to testify at the ICJ using this conditionality. Kagame had a second stroke of luck. His own government

---

67 Convention on the Prevention and Punishment of the Crime of Genocide. Adopted by the General Assembly of the United Nations on December 9, 1948, https://treaties.un.org/doc/publication/unts/volume%20 78/volume-78-i-1021-english.pdf.

68 ICJ, "Case Concerning Armed Activities on the Territory of the Congo (new application: 2002), Democratic Republic of the Congo *v.* Rwanda) Jurisdiction of the Court, Judgment of February 3, 2006, http://www.icj-cij.org/docket/ files/126/10435.pdf. See also http://reliefweb.int/report/democratic-republic-congo/icj-armed-activities-territory-congo-dr-congo-v-rwanda.

had passed "Décret-loi No. 014/01 of 15 February 1995," withdrawing the reservation entered by the Habyarimana regime. The decree meant that the new government had restored the ICJ's jurisdiction over Rwanda. That is where Kagame's second stroke of luck comes in. The publication of the decree by Rwanda did not, in itself, translate into the withdrawal of the Habyarimana reservation to Article IX of the Genocide Convention. Put in another way; the decree did not restore ICJ's jurisdiction over Rwanda. For that to happen, Rwanda had to submit a notification letter to the United Nations secretary-general confirming Rwanda's withdrawal of the 1975 reservation. Rwanda maintained to the ICJ that it never sent such a letter:

> Rwanda further observed that it had never notified withdrawal of its reservation to Article IX of the Genocide Convention to the United Nations Secretary-General, or taken any measure to withdraw it and that only such formal action on the international plane could constitute the definitive position of a State in regard to its treaty obligations.[69]

Kagame was off the hook. In an irony of ironies, Habyarimana saved Kagame from being held accountable for the killing fields in DRC. What Rwanda did is akin to taking the Fifth Amendment. According to the Fifth Amendment of the US Constitution, "No person shall be held to answer for a capital

---

69   Ibid.

or otherwise infamous crime…; nor shall be compelled in any criminal case to be a witness against himself."[70] Kagame's Rwanda understood very well that any utterances at the ICJ would be self-incriminating. Instead of engaging the court, as did the co-accused Uganda, Rwanda took the equivalent of the Fifth Amendment. In so doing, Rwanda successfully blocked the ICJ's jurisdiction.

To understand how Kagame entangled himself in DRC killings, we must revisit his own explanations of what motivated him to invade the country and what he thought he had achieved during his various interventions. Back on July 9, 1997, Kagame announced that the removal of Mobutu was part of his broader plan in a war that began in the eastern Congo, near the borders of Rwanda. He further revealed that the Rwandan forces led the capture of strategic regions and cities, including the Congolese capital, Kinshasa, the southern copper-mining town of Lubumbashi, and the diamond center of Kisangani. Kagame also admitted that Rwandan midlevel commanders trained and armed the Alliance of Democratic Forces for the Liberation of Congo-Zaire (ADFL) led by Laurent Kabila even before the campaign to overthrow Mobutu began. James Kabarebe, the general, currently serving as Rwandan defense minister, was in charge of the Congo military campaign, supported by other midlevel officers. To those who doubted Kagame's role in overthrowing a government and installing a new one,

---

70 Cornell University, Legal Information Institute, https://www.law.cornell.edu/wex/fifth_amendment.

he drove the point home in the following rather immodest terms:

> There are not many people who thought that Mobutu was very weak. They thought of Mobutu as a big monster who wouldn't be defeated, with his big hat and his big stick. They thought little Rwanda and big Zaire…Only when we started did they look at the map and see the possibilities.[71]

Kagame's battle plan had three main objectives: first, "dismantle" the Rwandan refugee camps in Congo that posed security risks for Rwanda; second, "destroy the structure" of the remnants of the old Rwandan state based in the camps either by "dealing with them here or scattering them"; and third, topple Mobutu. Kagame further explained that "These are some of the things we had to do. They may not be popular, but we are more interested in the results than with the stories about the results."[72] Kagame's version is collaborated by James Kabarebe and by General Kayumba Nyamwasa, at the time Rwanda's army chief of staff, who later became Kagame's victim. According to Kabarebe, Rwanda organized the Congolese into a movement with the goal of removing Mobutu from power:

---

71 Kagame Interview with John Pomfret, "Rwandans Led Revolt in Congo," Washington Post Foreign Service, July 9, 1997, http://www.washingtonpost.com/wp-srv/inatl/longterm/congo/stories/070997.htm.

72 Kagame Interview with John Pomfret, "Rwandans Led Revolt in Congo."

Among themselves, they did not know each other. Somebody from Rwanda had to help them meet... I introduced them to each other, and I introduced the agenda which was the liberation of Zaire and war against Mobutu...Rwanda provided the bulk of the troops.[73]

Nyamwasa agrees with this account. According to him, Rwanda's purpose was to put together different Congolese groups to "organize a political movement able to articulate a program, even justify the war going on in Congo."[74] That is how Rwanda entered Congo to "deal" with Rwandan refugees, overthrow a government, and install a new head of state. And just as in the case of the Rwandan genocide, Kagame was opposed to the international intervention in the refugee crisis, while claiming that the United Nations let down Rwanda and Congo by not intervening. In this case, too, he wanted to "solve" the problem on his own violent terms. Kagame quickly struck, before the multinational force being planned by Canadian, American, and British diplomats could become operational. Kagame attacked the Mugunga refugee camp and herded more than five hundred thousand refugees homeward back to Rwanda. Kagame even bragged about the green

---

73 James Kabarebe, "Rwandan Minister of Defense—Speaks of the Days He Was DRC Army Chief of Staff," https://www.youtube.com/watch?v=mECN7JSsnxY.

74 Kayumba Nyamwasa's interview in the documentary James Kabarebe, "Rwandan Minister of Defense—Speaks of the Days He Was DRC Army Chief of Staff," https://www.youtube.com/watch?v=mECN7JSsnxY.

light he had received from the United States, commending President Clinton's administration for "taking the right decisions to let it [invasion] proceed."[75] And off Kagame marched to topple Mobutu.

Under Kabarebe's command, the Rwandan military fought its way from Goma and Bukavu, on the eastern frontier of Congo, to the capital city of Kinshasa in the west—a distance of 2,679 km—to install Kabila into power in 1997. At the height of this campaign, Rwandan officers were de facto commanders of North Kivu, South Kivu, Orientale Province, and Equateur Province. The who's who in today's Rwandan Defense Forces (RDF) served in DRC, including General Caesar Kayizari, General Alex Kagame, General Patrick Nyamvumba, General Jack Nziza, and Colonel Dan Munyuza. Kagame's wars recall the words of the American General Colin Powell when cautioning the elder President Bush about invading Iraq. Powell's moral dictum, "If you break it, you own it," is very much applicable here. Kagame was soon to learn that the hard way.

On the fateful day of July 27, 1998, Kabila abruptly expelled Kabarebe and the Rwanda military, unleashing Kagame's anger and immediately expanding his killing fields. Kabila's dismissal orders went as follows:

The Supreme Commander of the Congolese National Armed Forces, the Head of State of the Republic of the Congo and the Minister of National Defense, advises the

---

75   Kagame interview with John Pomfret, "Rwandans Led Revolt in Congo."

Congolese people that he has just terminated, with effect from this Monday 27 July 1998, the Rwandan military presence which has assisted us during the period of the country's liberation. Through these military forces, he would like to thank all of the Rwandan people for the solidarity they have demonstrated to date. He would also like to congratulate the democratic Congolese people on their generosity of spirit for having tolerated, provided shelter for and trained these friendly forces during their stay in our country. This marks the end of the presence of all foreign military forces in the Congo.[76]

The ICJ offers a succinct account of how the Rwanda-DRC relationship deteriorated before being terminated on July 28, 1998:

Court observes that when President Kabila came to power, the influence of Uganda and in particular Rwanda in the DRC became substantial. In this context, it is worthy of note that many Rwandan officers held positions of high rank in the Congolese army and that Colonel James Kabarebe, of Rwandan nationality, was the Chief of Staff of the FAC (the armed forces of the DRC). From late spring 1998, President Kabila sought, for various reasons, to

76 Cited in International Court of Justice, Case Concerning Armed Activities on the Territory of the Congo, Democratic Republic of the Congo *v.* Uganda, Judgment of December 19, 2005, http://www.icj-cij.org/docket/files/116/10455.pdf. See also, http://www.iilj.org/wp-content/uploads/2016/08/Case-Concerning-Armed-Activities-on-the-Territory-of-the-Congo-Democratic-Republic-of-the-Congo-v.-Uganda-ICJ-2005.pdf

reduce this foreign influence; by mid-1998, relations between President Kabila and his former allies had deteriorated. In light of these circumstances, the presence of Rwandan troops on Congolese territory had, in particular, become a major concern for the Government of the DRC.[77]

Kabarebe provides details on how Rwanda's occupation of DRC collapsed. As he explains, Kabila accused Rwanda of looting Congo dry. "Kabila claimed we, Rwandans, were secretly smuggling…I immediately sent a report to Rwanda and Kabila went straight to Kigali" to confront the authorities.[78] The United Nations was also dealing with the issue of the exploitation of the DRC's mineral resources by its occupiers.[79] In Kigali, Laurent Kabila told his Rwandan sponsors that "we have forged bonds between friendship and brotherhood. But friendship must be maintained. And we must have mutual respect." Later, Laurent Kabila advised his senior military officers that the Rwandans came to Congo as conquerors:

These gentlemen found so much honey here…They do not want to leave this country. If only they could stay in this country while respecting the indigenous inhabitants. We would accept them easily. But they

77   Ibid.

78   Kabarebe, "Rwandan Minister of Defense."

79   UN Security Council, "Security Council Condemns Illegal Exploitation of Democratic Republic of Congo's Natural Resources," May 3, 2001, http://www.un.org/press/en/2001/sc7057.doc.htm.

came as conquerors to dominate everyone. This is unacceptable.[80]

Kagame's response to Kabila's expulsion of the Rwandan military was predictable—a new terror campaign to remove Kabila. Under the command of the same Kabarebe, the Rwandan military commandeered a civilian aircraft from Goma and flew west to seize Kitona airfield near the Atlantic coast. The next phase of the mission was to overrun the DRC's capital, Kinshasa, and remove Kabila from power. That is what Kagame is famous for—immense military acumen that combines audacity, surprise, and speed to overwhelm the enemy.

Kagame's scheme turned into an utter disaster for him and DRC. Kagame's army was decimated by Angolan and Zimbabwean armies enlisted by Kabila to save his regime. That is how Kagame ignited the second Congo war, drawing in several African armies. According to the US government, "An estimated five million people have died in the years since the second regional war began in 1998, and millions more have been forced to flee their homes."[81]

Ironically, one of the bloodiest episodes after Kabila's expulsion of the Rwandan military resulted from the fallout

---

80 Laurent Kabila in the documentary "Kabarebe, Rwandan Minister of Defense."

81 Testimony by Johnnie Carson, Assistant Secretary, Bureau of African Affairs, as Prepared Before the House Committee on Foreign Affairs Subcommittee on Africa, Global Health, and Human Rights, December 11, 2012, https://2009-2017.state.gov/p/af/rls/rm/2012/201812.htm.

between the former allies—Rwanda and Uganda. The two co-occupiers clashed for control of DRC's third-largest city, Kisangani, in 1999–2000, fighting for no less than three battles. Reporting on the third battle, the United Nations Inter-Agency Mission concluded:

> The city of Kisangani is one of the worst casualties of the most complex war in Africa…On 5 June, persisting tensions in Kisangani between the occupying forces of Uganda and Rwanda erupted into open and violent conflict, with fighting spreading into residential areas and indiscriminate shelling occurring for six days. It was the third and by far the most brutal clash between the two armies battling to control the city, for reasons their leaders could never adequately explain. This has led some observers to suspect that an underlying cause was control of the lucrative diamond industry. Over 760 civilians were killed, and an estimated 1,700 wounded. More than 4,000 houses were partially damaged, destroyed or made uninhabitable. Sixty-nine schools were shelled, and other public buildings were badly damaged. Medical facilities and the cathedral were also damaged during the shelling, and 65,000 residents were forced to flee the fighting and seek refuge in nearby forests.[82]

---

82 UN Security Council, "Report of the Inter-agency Assessment Mission to Kisangani," December 5, 2000, http://reliefweb.int/report/democratic-republic-congo/report-inter-agency-assessment-mission-kisangani.

The US government made a similar conclusion about Kisangani's destruction, noting that both Rwandan and Ugandan "forces shelled the city with artillery and mortar fire, destroying homes and much of the city's infrastructure."[83]

After barely one year in power, Laurent Kabila was now facing a grim situation. The United Nations' demands that Rwanda and Uganda leave DRC were falling on deaf ears. The UN Security Council condemned "all massacres and other atrocities carried out in Congolese territory," and "urged that an international investigation be held with a view to bringing those responsible to justice." The Council further demanded that Rwandan and Ugandan forces "withdraw immediately and completely from the city of Kisangani."[84] Neither Uganda nor Rwanda heeded to the withdrawal calls—they dug in instead, intent on occupying different parts of DRC.

Upon the assassination of President Laurent Kabila in January 2001, his son Joseph Kabila took over the presidency and attempted a different strategy for ending Rwandan and Ugandan occupation. DRC took Rwanda and Uganda to the ICJ in 2002. The case against Rwanda included the following crimes:

---

83 US Department of State, "Rwanda—Country Reports on Human Rights Practices 2000," 2001, https://www.state.gov/j/drl/rls/hrrpt/2000/af/720.htm.

84 Security Council, "Security Council Demands that Ugandan and Rwandan Forces Withdraw Immediately from Kisangani, Democratic Republic of Congo," June 16, 2000, http://www.un.org/press/en/2000/20000616.sc6877.doc.html.

[B]y engaging in killing, slaughter, rape, throat-slitting, and crucifying, Rwanda is guilty of genocide against more than 3,500,000 Congolese, including the victims of the recent massacres in the city of Kisangani, and has violated the sacred right to life provided for in the Universal Declaration of Human Rights and in the International Covenant on Civil and Political Rights, the Convention on the Prevention and Punishment of the Crime of Genocide and other relevant international legal instruments; In consequence, and in accordance with the international legal obligations referred to above, to adjudge and declare that: (1) all Rwandan armed forces at the origin of the aggression shall forthwith quit the territory of the Democratic Republic of the Congo, so as to enable the Congolese people to enjoy in full their rights to peace, to security, to their resources and to development; (2) Rwanda is under an obligation to procure the immediate, unconditional withdrawal of its armed forces and the like from Congolese territory; (3) the Democratic Republic of the Congo is entitled to compensation from Rwanda for all acts of looting, destruction, slaughter, removal of property or persons and other acts of wrongdoing imputable to Rwanda, in respect of which the Democratic Republic of the Congo reserves the right to establish a precise assessment

of the prejudice at a later date, in addition to resti-
tution of the property removed.[85]

The charges against Uganda included:

Finds that the Republic of Uganda, by acts of looting, plundering and exploitation of Congolese natural resources committed by members of the Ugandan
armed forces in the territory of the Democratic
Republic of the Congo and by its failure to comply
with its obligations as an occupying Power in Ituri
district to prevent acts of looting, plundering and
exploitation of Congolese natural resources, violated
obligations owed to the Democratic Republic of the
Congo under international law.[86]

The ICJ ruled against Uganda but not Rwanda. In the case of
Uganda, the court determined that:

In its Judgment, which is final, binding and without
appeal, the Court (1) By sixteen votes to one, Finds

---

85   ICJ, The Democratic Republic of the Congo initiates proceedings against
Rwanda citing massive human rights violations by Rwanda on Congolese territory The Democratic Republic of the Congo requests the Court to indicate pro-
visional measures as a matter of urgency THE HAGUE, 28 May 2002, http://
www.icj-cij.org/files/case-related/126/126-20020528-PRE-01-00-EN.pdf.

86   ICJ, "Armed activities on the territory of the Congo (Democratic Republic of
the Congo *v.* Uganda)," http://reliefweb.int/report/democratic-republic-congo/
armed-activities-territory-congo-democratic-republic-congo-v-uganda;

that the Republic of Uganda, by engaging in military activities against the Democratic Republic of the Congo on the latter's territory, by occupying Ituri and by actively extending military, logistic, economic and financial support to irregular forces having operated on the territory of the DRC, violated the principle of non-use of force in international relations and the principle of non-intervention.[87]

The court ordered Uganda to make reparations for its role in acts of looting, killing and torturing the Congolese people and the destruction of property and infrastructure. In the court's own words, "given the character of the internationally wrongful acts for which Uganda has been found responsible, the Court considers that those acts resulted in injury to the DRC and to persons on its territory. Consequently, the Court finds that Uganda has an obligation to make reparation for the injury caused."[88]

But the case against Rwanda could not even advance to trial. As previously noted, the ICJ had no jurisdiction over Rwanda, thanks to the Habyarimana regime's reservation on the Genocide Convention. The court concluded that Rwanda's statement that it "is not, and never has been, party to the 1984 Convention against Torture," was found that to be "indeed the case." For this reason, the court "finds that it

---

87 ICJ, "Armed activities on the territory of the Congo (Democratic Republic of the Congo v. Uganda)," http://reliefweb.int/report/democratic-republic-congo/armed-activities-territory-congo-democratic-republic-congo-v-uganda.
88 Ibid.

has no jurisdiction to entertain the Application filed by the Democratic Republic of the Congo on 28 May 2002."[89]

The court, however, made a fundamental statement about Rwanda's behavior. The court stressed that it reached "this conclusion solely in the context of the preliminary question of whether it has jurisdiction in this case." The court was, therefore "precluded by its Statute from taking any position on the merits of the claims made by the DRC." However,

> [A]s the Court has stated on numerous previous occasions, there is a fundamental distinction between the question of the acceptance by States of the Court's jurisdiction and the conformity of their acts with international law. Whether or not States have accepted the jurisdiction of the Court, they are required to fulfill their obligations under the United Nations Charter and the other rules of international law, including international humanitarian and human rights law, and they remain responsible for acts attributable to them which are contrary to international law.[90]

Expecting Kagame to accept international laws is rather farfetched. This is a head of state who refers to international

---

89 ICJ, Case Concerning Armed Activities on the Territory of the Congo (new application: 2002), Democratic Republic of the Congo. Rwanda) Jurisdiction of the Court, Judgment of February 3, 2006, http://www.icj-cij.org/docket/files/126/10435.pdf.

90 Ibid.

justice as "nonsense."[91] In fact, Kagame moved in the opposite direction, even accusing the United Nations itself of practicing genocide denial and double genocide ideologies. For example, when in 2010 the United Nations DRC mapping exercise report called for an investigation to determine whether the atrocities committed by Rwanda in DRC constituted genocide, Rwanda accused the authors of the report of committing genocide crimes. According to the Kagame government, "The desire to validate the double genocide theory is consistently present throughout the [mapping]…report by 'mirror-imaging' the actors, ideology, and methods employed during the 1994 Rwandan genocide." The Kagame government then concluded that the relationship between Rwanda and the DRC "is the strongest and healthiest it has been in decades."[92] Of course, we know that two years later, the Rwanda-sponsored M23 militia overran the provincial capital of Goma, with most donor countries suspending aid to Rwanda.

---

91 Speech by President Kagame at the 17th Genocide Commemoration Ceremony, Kigali, April 7, 2011, http://www.paulkagame.com/index.php/speeches/314-president-kagame-speech-at-the-17th-commemoration-of-the-genocide-against-the-tutsis-kigali-7th-april-2011.

92 Republic of Rwanda, "Official government of Rwanda comments on the draft UN mapping exercise report on the DRC," October 30, 2010, http://www.ohchr.org/Documents/Countries/CD/DRC_Report_Comments_Rwanda.pdf.

CHAPTER 5

Kagame's Confrontations
with African States

―――

KAGAME HAS FOUGHT EVERY NEIGHBORING state besides DRC. And the cause of the conflict is mainly one thing—death of Rwandans who fled their homeland into exile in neighboring states. Kagame's first major confrontation was with Kenya. Rwanda–Kenya diplomatic relations were severed in 1996 due to an attempted assassination of the exiled former Rwandan minister, Seth Sendashonga. Before breaking off diplomatic relations, Kenya gave Rwanda two choices—either waive the diplomatic immunity of the envoy caught at the crime scene so he could be tried for attempted assassination of Sendashonga, or close the Rwandan embassy and leave Kenya. Rwanda refused to relinquish the diplomatic immunity. Its embassy was shut down, while Kenya also closed its embassy in Rwanda. Two years later, Sendashonga was murdered in the Kenyan capital of Nairobi. It took four years for the two countries to normalize their relations.

Ironically, the motivation for reestablishing relations between Rwanda and Kenya came from another conflict involving Kagame. While Kenya and Rwanda were reviving their diplomatic relations in July 2000 with Kagame's visit to Kenya—reciprocating President Daniel Moi's visit to Rwanda—the latter had clashed with Uganda in DRC in June 2000. The Rwandan and Ugandan armies had just destroyed much of Kisangani, in the process displacing over sixty thousand, killing nearly eight hundred, and injuring seventeen hundred. In addition to Kenya's attempt at mediation was the British effort—in particular, that of the aid minister Claire Short, who in 2001 brokered talks that averted a direct war between Rwanda and Uganda. The famous leaked letter from President Museveni to Short provides insight into what was going on between Rwanda and Uganda:

> We have had to stand by Rwanda in Congo although they do not seem to show any appreciation for the sacrifice…given that Kagame is turning the sister state of Uganda into an enemy state of Uganda, we cannot go on with hamstrung position of having a small, under-equipped Army in such a volatile situation… I need to inform you that Rwanda currently has an Army of 100,000 officers and men. They maintain this big Army by, apparently, not paying wages for soldiers in Congo…It is possibly this level of manpower that gives them the arrogance to think that they can interfere in the internal affairs of Uganda.

This in addition to the ideological bankruptcy of their leadership I have had the occasion to mention to you.[93]

Rwanda and Uganda did not go to war, thanks in large part to Short's intervention.

The next Kagame confrontations involved South Africa and Tanzania. In the case of South Africa, several exiled senior Rwandan officials found sanctuary there, including former army chief of staff Kayumba Nyamwasa and former intelligence chief Patrick Karegeya. Colonel Karegeya was murdered on December 31, 2013, while Nyamwasa survived several assassination attempts between 2010 and 2014. By May 2014, South Africa had expelled all Rwandan diplomats, excepting the ambassador. In the case of the failed assassination of Nyamwasa, a South African court pronounced the following as it sentenced several would-be-assassins that included Rwandan nationals:

I have stated in my judgment that you did not know the victim. Your motive for shooting him was for personal gain. You committed the offenses out of greed after you were paid a certain amount of money. You are not the main culprits in this matter...The attempted murder of General Kayumba Nyamwasa

93 President Yoweri Museveni to UK development secretary Claire Short, http://www.therwandan.com/blog/president-museveni-kagames-leadership-ideologically-bankrupt-2001/.

was therefore politically motivated. Emanating from a certain group of people from Rwanda.[94]

The amount of money offered to the assassins was US$1 million. The court documents state that "the accused offered to give $1,000,000 to police officers, according to their evidence."[95] Robert Higiro, a former army captain in the Rwandan army, also testified in the US Congress that he, too, had been offered US$1 million to assassinate Nyamwasa.[96]

Tanzania was next. Kagame verbally attacked Tanzanian head of state Jakaya Kikwete after the latter suggested that Rwanda should negotiate with its many adversaries at home and abroad. In Kagame's own words: "I won't even discuss it because I will just wait for you at the right place and I will hit you."[97] In August 2013, the two presidents were to find themselves on opposite sides of the DRC conflict. Kagame was accused of arming the militia M23 that had overrun the regional capital of Goma, while Kikwete supplied troops to neutralize the militia as a fighting force. Under the command of a Tanzanian general, a UN intervention brigade consisting

---

94 The case of Kayumba Nyamwasa, Court Case No 41/1325/2010, 2014/-08-29, In the Regional Court for the Regional Division of South Gauteng Held at Kagiso, Presiding Officer, Stanley Mkhari.

95 Ibid.

96 Testimony of Robert Higiro Subcommittee on Africa, Global Health, Global Human Rights, and International Organizations US House of Representatives May 20, 2015, http://docs.house.gov/meetings/FA/FA16/20150520/103498/HHRG-114-FA16-Wstate-HigiroR-20150520.pdf.

97 Transcript of Paul Kagame Address at Youth CONNEKT Dialogue, Kigali, June 30, 2013, http://www.paulkagame.com/index.php/speeches/1150-transcript-of-he-paul-kagame-address-at-youth-connekt-dialogue.

of troops from Tanzania, South Africa, and Malawi successfully disarmed M23.[98] Most of the M23 fighters repatriated to, and detained in Rwanda but soon mysteriously "vanished" with official connivance. The United States government describes how this happened:

> In 2013 the government disarmed approximately 770 March 23 Movement Congolese rebel combatants who crossed into the country from the DRC and detained them in a converted police training facility in Ngoma. As in previous years, detainees left or escaped the Ngoma internment center, and the government was unable to account for their whereabouts. In September observers reported there were approximately 100 detainees in the internment center, a substantial decrease from the nearly 400 individuals interned in the center at the end of 2015; 29 of the former combatants were positively identified among the refugee population in the country's five Congolese camps.[99]

The latest Kagame confrontation with an African state involved Burundi in 2015–2016. Kagame verbally attacked the

98 United Nations Organization Stabilization Mission in DR Congo, "Last Batch of Tanzanian Troops Now in Goma for the Force Intervention Brigade," June 14, 2013, https://monusco.unmissions.org/en/last-batch-tanzanian-troops-now-goma-force-intervention-brigade.

99 US Department of State, "Rwanda—Country Reports on Human Rights Practices 2016," 2017, https://www.state.gov/documents/organization/265502.pdf

Burundian president, Pierre Nkurunziza, for seeking a third presidential term. Kagame proclaimed that Nkurunziza was not fit to govern and should not change the constitution to stay in power after serving two terms. Ironically, that is what Kagame himself did. In Kagame's own words: "If your own citizens are telling you we don't want you to do this or to lead us, it is because they are saying you are not delivering much to us. So how do you say I am staying anyway whether you want me or not? This is a serious problem."[100] The US Department of State's 2015 human-rights report referred to the recruitment of Burundian refugees based in Rwanda into militias seeking to overthrow Nkurunziza:

> Other major human rights problems reported included arbitrary or unlawful killings; torture and harsh conditions in prisons and detention centers; arbitrary arrest; prolonged pretrial detention…the alleged recruitment of Burundian-origin refugees, including possibly some children, to serve in armed groups in Burundi.[101]

Kagame's violence went global—Britain and Sweden. The 2011 US Department of State's report on Rwanda highlighted

---

100 Edwin Musoni, "Kagame Speaks Out on Burundi Political Crisis," *The New Times*, May 9, 2015, http://www.newtimes.co.rw/section/article/2015-05-09/188624/.

101 US Department of State, "Rwanda—Country Reports on Human Rights Practices 2015," 2016, https://www.state.gov/documents/organization/252929.pdf.

the following: "United Kingdom police in May warned specific Rwandan exiles in London that they were the targets of an assassination plot by the Rwandan government."[102] In February 2012, the second in command of the Rwandan embassy in Sweden was expelled for engaging in what was termed "refugee espionage."[103]

The irrationality of Kagame's confrontation with Kenya, Uganda, Tanzania, and South Africa is illustrated by Rwanda's economic and trading circumstances. Rwanda is doubly landlocked. To reach the seaport of Mombasa in Kenya, which is Rwanda's main gateway to regional and international trade, Rwandan exports and imports have to pass through Uganda and Kenya. The alternative transit corridor is Tanzania and its seaport of Dar-Es-Salaam. But Kagame was fighting with each of these countries—to the extent of total diplomatic breakdown with Kenya. Furthermore, South Africa is Africa's trading and education hub, with hundreds of Rwandans regularly doing business and studying in the major cities of Johannesburg, Cape Town, and Durban. The expulsion of their respective diplomats was tantamount to Kagame shooting himself in the foot—South Africa no longer processes visas in Rwanda. To acquire visas into South Africa, Rwandans must travel to neighboring countries.

---

102 US Department of State, "Rwanda—Country Reports on Human Rights Practices 2011," 2012, https://www.state.gov/documents/organization/186443.pdf.

103 PRI, "Sweden Expels Rwanda Diplomat for Spying," February 13, 2012, https://www.pri.org/stories/2012-02-13/rwanda-news-sweden-expels-rwanda-diplomat-spying.

CHAPTER 6

Kagame's Fierce Critic and Financier:
The Case of the United States

────

ON MAY 20, 2015, THE US principal deputy assistant secretary of state for African Affairs, Robert Jackson, gave a startling testimony about Rwanda in the US Congress. Jackson stated that the American government publicly expressed concern "about the succession of what appeared to be politically motivated killings of government critics in exile." Jackson added that the United States had "expressed concern in June 2014 about the arrest, incommunicado detentions, and disappearances of scores of Rwandan citizens; in September 2014 we called for an independent investigation of the bodies found in July and August in Lake Rweru, which sits astride the Rwanda-Burundi border."[104] Deputy assistant secretary

─────────

104   Assistant Secretary Robert P. Jackson's testimony before the House Foreign Affairs Committee Subcommittee on Africa, Global Health, Global Human Rights, and International Organizations, May 20, 2015, http://docs. house.gov/meetings/FA/FA16/20150520/103498/HHRG-114-FA16-Wstate-JacksonR-20150520.pdf.

Steve Feldstein's testimony was even more astounding. He stated that the US government had for years engaged Kagame himself on these serious charges:

> We have articulated our concerns about Rwanda's human rights record for years directly to Rwanda's senior leaders, *including President Kagame*, and we have highlighted the deteriorating situation in Rwanda, through the State Department's annual human rights report. The Department's 2013 human rights report for Rwanda… highlighted reports that arbitrary or unlawful killings took place both inside and outside Rwanda.[105]

Three years earlier, Ambassador Susan Rice, the then-US permanent representative to the United Nations, had raised the same concerns on her visit to Rwanda: "The political culture in Rwanda remains comparatively closed. Press restrictions persist. Civil society activists, journalists, and political opponents of the government often fear organizing peacefully and speaking out. Some have been harassed. Some have been intimidated by late-night callers. Some have simply disappeared."[106]

---

105 Deputy Assistant Secretary Steve Feldstein Bureau of Democracy, Human Rights and Labor before the Subcommittee on Africa, Global Health, Global Human Rights and International Organizations May 20, 2015 (italics added), http://docs.house.gov/meetings/FA/FA16/20150520/103498/HHRG-114-FA16-Wstate-FeldsteinS-20150520.pdf.

106 Remarks by Ambassador Susan E. Rice, US Permanent Representative to the United Nations, at the Kigali Institute of Science and Technology on "Building a New Nation: Rwanda's Progress and Potential," November 23, 2011, https://2009-2017-usun.state.gov/remarks/5249.

These statements by senior American government officials about atrocities and disappearances in Rwanda highlight the contradictory relationship between the two countries. The United States is both the leading critic of Rwanda and a tenacious supporter of the Kagame government. This inconsistency was aptly noted by the Chairman of the House Foreign Affairs Committee, Ed Royce when calling for a reassessment of relations between the United States and Rwanda:

> While I am cognizant of the strategic role Rwanda's security forces play in peacekeeping missions throughout the continent, this should not blind us to the regime's attempts to violently close the political space for opposition voices. As we prepare to mark the twenty-year anniversary of the genocide in Rwanda…the friends of Rwanda must ensure that we do not, once again, miss the warning signs of political dysfunction and repression.[107]

The Chairman of the House Subcommittee on Africa, Health, Global Human Rights, and International Organizations, Chris Smith, also expressed his disappointment about the US support to Kagame despite his violence:

---

107 US Congress, Foreign Affairs Committee, "Chairman Royce Decries Targeted Killings of Rwandan Regime Critics Abroad," https://foreignaffairs.house.gov/press-release/chairman-royce-decries-targeted-killings-of-rwandan-regime-critics-abroad/.

Kagame has been considered a hero on the international stage, and has long been immune to public criticism...[T]here are credible reports that the RPF government has commissioned assassins to kill dissidents...By largely avoiding criticism of Rwandan human rights issues, the Bush and Obama administrations raised appropriations to Rwanda from $39 million in FY2003 to $188 million in FY2014.[108]

The strong American statements about Kagame's carnage notwithstanding, the United States has been, and remains, at the forefront of support for the Rwandan state, including capacity-building of the Rwandan military. American support may be measured in both soft and hard terms. In the "soft" supporting role, the United States has consistently turned a blind eye to Kagame's military adventurism in DRC. American "hard" support is very much evident in building the capacity of the Rwandan military. From the presidencies of Bill Clinton, George W. Bush, and Barack Obama, each administration has invested significantly in the Rwandan military. Whether it was a Republican or Democratic presidency, the United States consistently poured millions of dollars into Rwanda's military machine.

The building of the Rwandan military by the United States can be traced from immediately after the genocide

---

108 Hon. Christopher H. Smith, 'Developments in Rwanda," Congressional Record, Thursday, May 21, 2015, https://www.congress.gov/congressional-record/2015/05/21/extensions-of-remarks-section/article/E787-2

ended. Bill Clinton, who had opposed intervention to stop genocide, turned into an enthusiast for building the RPF army. From July 30 to September 30, 1994, the US military established a twenty-four-hour expanded air logistics site at Kigali International Airport. After the rehabilitation of the airport, Kigali served as a hub for all relief flights in support of humanitarian operations. According to the US Department of Defense, at the height of the operation, there was about two hundred military personnel in Kigali.[109] The next phase was demining Kigali and the rest of the country. The US Department of Defense indicates that from July 18 to August 30, 1995, thirty-five military personnel established the National Demining Office, training 120 Rwandan military personnel. The Americans also provided demining equipment, medical supplies, off-the-shelf communications equipment, and other support materials to the newly established Rwandan demining body.

And then came the training of the Rwandan soldiers. During the period from July 15 to August 30, 1996, the US military trained "RPA soldiers with a focus on small unit leader training, tactical skills, land navigation, first aid, and basic rifle marksmanship." The basic rifle marksmanship training was conducted "at the Gabiro training area in eastern Rwanda and included familiarization and qualification of assigned weapons." Next came the training of Rwandan civilian and military personnel "in operations to assist repatriation of refugees and other displaced

---

109 US Department of Defense, "Report to Congress on US Military Activities in Rwanda, 1994," August 1997, http://www.dod.gov/pubs/rwanda/summary.html.

civilians." When the thousands of the refugees pushed into Rwanda from Congo in 1996, the American military was right there, assisting and training the Rwandan military with "planning and conducting public information campaigns supporting refugee repatriation and reintegration." The US Department of Defense insists, however, that the return of the thousands of refugees from Congo and the presence of American military personnel was coincidental. As the Department explains:

> Coincidentally, the [US] teams deployed to Rwanda about two weeks before the mass repatriation from Zaire...The team then conducted five days of practical exercises which included visits to the border at Gisenyi, and assessments of a UNHCR camp for returning refugees and of a commune level transit camp.[110]

The training of the Rwandan military continued and expanded to the senior ranks. In the period from July 15 to August 30, 1997, the US military trained RPA on leadership at Gako in Rwanda. The course included "training in the law of war and human rights, military leadership, decision-making, personnel and equipment maintenance, and soldier team development."[111] What we see here is that the United States was training the Rwandan military while the latter was invading DRC. The irony was that among the objectives of training the Rwandan military was mak-

---

110 Ibid.
111 Ibid.

ing RPA "respect" human rights. The Rwandan military was doing the opposite.

In building the Rwandan military, the US government advanced four objectives: "develop capacity of the military as a non-political, professional force respectful of human rights; enhance ability to participate in peacekeeping operations; develop its NCO academy; and enhance capacity to maintain territorial integrity and secure uncontrolled waters in the Great Lakes region." The United States, for example, spent US$2,678,381 to implement these objectives in Rwanda in 2011.[112] For 2015, the purpose of the American support to the Rwandan military was said to include the following: "military professionalization; adherence to norms of human rights; civilian control of the military; and peacekeeping." The United States spent US$2,125,631 on these programs in 2015.[113]

These training programs are by no means the only channels through which the United States has assisted in building the Rwandan military. For the bigger picture, we have to look closely at the George W. Bush administration. It was during this period the Rwandan military got an even more significant attention from the United States. This is when Rwanda's military became one of the leading peacekeeping forces in the world. Kagame understood that peacekeeping is big business. For example, the United States approved

---

112   The United States Department of Defense, and the United States Department of State, "Foreign Military Training Fiscal Years 2011 and 2012, Joint Report to Congress Volume I," https://www.state.gov/documents/organization/197595.pdf.

113   Ibid.

US$7.87 billion to support the operations of the peacekeeping personnel in 2016–2017. Rwanda's peacekeeping troops are significant—6,137 Rwandans, or 5.7 percent of 107,574 peacekeeping personnel in 2016–2017.[114] The UN reimburses countries volunteering uniformed personnel to peacekeeping operations at a rate of a little over US$1,332 per soldier per month.[115] For Kagame, involvement increased his global prestige, not to mention earning free training and experience for his military.

Peacekeeping brought Kagame even closer to the United States, which is by far the largest financial contributor to peacekeeping at nearly 30 percent. Unwilling to put American soldiers in combat theaters in Africa proved to be a win-win for both the United States and Rwanda. This was especially so during the administration of George W. Bush, who appeared to be a genuine admirer of Kagame. Bush's description of Kagame in 2006 says it all:

> The President is—he's a man of action, he can get things done. I'm proud of your leadership. We have talked about a lot of issues. We talked about the Sudan, and I want to thank the President for committing troops in the AU mission to help deal with

---

114 The United Nations, "Peacekeeping Fact Sheet," as of April 30, 2017, http://www.un.org/en/peacekeeping/resources/statistics/factsheet.shtml.

115 The United Nations, http://www.un.org/en/peacekeeping/operations/financing.shtml.

what I have called a genocide. We strategized about how we can go forward to resolve the situation.[116]

On his visit to Rwanda in 2008, President George W. Bush was to praise Kagame even more, highlighting millions of dollars his government had earmarked for building the Rwandan military:

And the United States is happy to help. We've trained—or helped train more than 7,000 Rwanda peacekeepers. We've provided more than $17 million to equip and transport these forces into Darfur. The President mentioned something that I agree with, and that is, the role of the United States and others is to help African nations deal with African problems... The United States is making $100 million available to assist African nations willing to step forward for the cause of peace in Darfur, and up to $12 million of those will help you, Mr. President, do the job that you want to do in Darfur.[117]

Talking directly about the DRC, George W. Bush thanked Kagame for his work there: "The United States and Rwanda

116   US White House, "President Bush Welcomes President Kagame of Rwanda to the White House," May 31, 2006, https://georgewbush-whitehouse.archives.gov/news/releases/2006/05/20060531-1.html.

117   US White House, "President Bush Participates in Joint Press Availability with President Kagame of Rwanda," February 19, 2008, https://georgewbush-whitehouse.archives.gov/news/releases/2008/02/20080219-6.html.

are cooperating to assure long-term stability in eastern Congo...I appreciate your guidance and your advice, Mr. President."[118] In praising Kagame for stabilizing DRC, George W. Bush was stretching the truth, to say the least.

Not much changed during the Obama presidency. In 2014, the United States launched the US$110 million per year for three to five years, to build the capability of leading African militaries. The program supported "military training, equipment maintenance and repair, institutional support, and interoperability with other Africa-based peacekeeping forces." The Rwandan military prominently featured in this Obama program.[119] Only once did the United States take a concrete action against Kagame's militarism in DRC. On December 11, 2012, the assistant secretary of state for African affairs, Johnnie Carson, shared the American frustration in a testimony on "The Devastating Crisis in Eastern Congo":

> [W]e continue to press Rwanda to halt and prevent any and all forms of support to Congolese armed groups. As required by law, the Department suspended Foreign Military Financing funds to Rwanda this year. Looking forward, we expect all parties, including Rwanda, to cease any support to M23 and other armed groups..., and to work constructively

---

118 Ibid.

119 Obama Whitehouse, "Fact Sheet on US Support for Peacekeeping in Africa," https://obamawhitehouse.archives.gov/the-press-office/2014/08/06/fact-sheet-us-support-peacekeeping-africa.

with neighbors and the international community and take affirmative steps to end impunity for M23 commanders responsible for human rights abuses in order to reach an acceptable political agreement.[120]

The US government's subsequent records indicate how negligible this action against Rwanda, and indeed, how soon it was reversed in Kagame's favor. In 2011, American foreign military training support to Rwanda amounted to US$2,678,381.[121] When sanctioned for supporting M23, the American support for training the Rwandan military dropped to US$1,434,010 in 2012.[122] In 2013, the military support increased to US$1,664,895.[123] The amount yet increased again in 2014 to US$2,122,029,[124] reaching US$2,125,631 in 2015.[125] In other words, it was business as usual.

120   Testimony Assistant Secretary Johnnie Carson Bureau of African Affairs US Department of State Before the House Committee on Foreign Affairs Subcommittee on Africa, Global Health and Human Rights, "The Devastating Crisis in Eastern Congo," December 11, 2012, http://archives.republicans.foreignaffairs.house.gov/112/HHRG-112-FA16-WState-CarsonJ-20121211.pdf.

121   United States Department of State, "Foreign Military Training and DoD Engagement Activities of Interest," 2011, https://www.state.gov/documents/organization/197603.pdf.

122   United States Department of State, "Foreign Military Training and DoD Engagement Activities of Interest," https://www.state.gov/documents/organization/213452.pdf.

123   Ibid.

124   Ibid.

125   Ibid.

The established pattern in the United States–Rwanda military relationship is clear. The American government keeps denouncing Rwanda's atrocities year after year. Among the atrocities denounced by the United States in 2015 were "security forces' disregard for the rule of law; and restrictions on civil liberties." Other major human-rights abuses in Rwanda in 2015 were "arbitrary or unlawful killings; torture and harsh conditions in prisons and detention centers."[126] There is nothing new in these atrocities. Meanwhile, the United States' funding for reinforcing Kagame's security forces increases.

---

126   US Department of State, "Rwanda—Country Reports on Human Rights Practices 2015," 2016, https://www.state.gov/documents/organization/252929.pdf.

CHAPTER 7

Kagame's Capitalism without Capitalists

DURING THE TWENTY-SEVENTH AFRICAN UNION (AU) summit in Kigali in July 2016, President Kagame was tasked with reforming the AU Commission into a self-financing and dynamic entity able to cater to the needs of the continent's population of 1.2 billion. The self-financing formula calls for member states to raise US$1.2 billion annually to finance AU activities. Kagame has explained the five tasks of his reform agenda as follows:

> First, the African Union will focus on key priorities with continental scope, while empowering Regional Economic Communities to take the lead where they are best placed to do so. Second, re-align African Union Institutions to deliver on those key priorities. Third, connect the African Union more closely to citizens, so our people feel they have a stake in its work.

Fourth, manage the business of the African Union more efficiently and effectively...Finally, finance the African Union sustainably from our own resources.[127]

The history of Africa's grand projects is not very good. In the case of the Lagos Plan of Action launched in 1980, African governments stated, "We commit ourselves, individually and collectively, on behalf of our governments and peoples, to establish national, sub-regional and regional institutions which will facilitate the attainment of objectives of self-reliance and self-sustainment."[128] In adopting the New Partnership for Africa's Development (NEPAD) in 2001, African leaders agreed "to eradicate poverty and to place their countries, both individually and collectively, on a path of sustainable growth and development, and at the same time to participate actively in the world economy."[129] Both the Lagos Action Plan and NEPAD came into being with a big bang but were soon forgotten.

The Kagame-led grand agenda will most likely go the same way. His qualification to lead Africa is his purported

---

127 Paul Kagame, "Remarks by President Kagame: Meeting on Institutional Reform of the African Union," April 24, 2017, http://paulkagame.com/index.php/speeches/1824-remarks-by-president-paul-kagame-meeting-on-institutional-reform-of-the-african-union-conakry-24-april-2017.

128 The Organization of African Unity, "Lagos Plan of Action for the Economic Development of Africa 1980–2000," file:///H:/Lagos-Plan-of-Action%20(1).pdf.

129 "The New Partnership for Africa's Development Action Plan," 2003, file:///H:/Actionplan-Nepad-English-Publication%20(2).pdf.

socioeconomic transformation of Rwanda. Give Kagame his credit. He travels far and wide to tell global audiences how he turned Rwanda into an African economic lion by learning from the Asian economic tigers.[130] His audiences appear to believe him, proving once again that "if you tell a lie big enough and keep repeating it, people will eventually come to believe it."[131]

The problem is the type of capitalism Kagame has built. It is a form of capitalism in which the capitalists are endangered species. Their businesses are illegally seized without compensation. They flee the country—and in some cases mysteriously die. The violence that has affected other segments of the Rwandan society has not spared the Rwandan business community.

One of the earliest victims was Valens Kajeguhakwa and his bank, Banque Continentale Africaine du Rwanda (BACAR). Kajeguhakwa, his two sons, and the entire senior management were charged in 2001 for allegedly misappropriating the equivalent of US$2.4 million. The government of Rwanda claimed that these crimes were committed between 1994 and 2001. But the Rwanda National Commission for Human Rights (RNCHR), which was still relatively functional during the BACAR case in the early 2000s—and kept records—indicated otherwise. From the RNCHR's records,

130 Paul Kagame, "Rwanda and the New Lions of Africa," The Wall Street Journal, May 19, 2013 https://www.wsj.com/articles/SB10001424127887324767004578485234078541160.

131 Joseph Goebbels, "Jewish Virtual Library," http://www.jewishvirtual-library.org/joseph-goebbels-on-the-quot-big-lie-quot.

we get an insight into how the Rwanda government manipulated the justice system to drive Kajeguhakwa out of business.

On September 21, 2001, the entire BACAR senior management staff was detained for thirty days. The detention was extended for another thirty days. Imprisoned managers lodged an appeal with the Supreme Court against the warrants of their detention—their case was heard on November 21, 2001. The Supreme Court ordered the senior managers to be released on November 23. But the prosecutor's office failed to implement the release decision until December 11, 2001. When they were released, they were immediately arrested again. The appeal hearing did not take place until February 17, 2002.

Observing this legal thuggery, the RCNHR concluded that the "re-arrest of the accused amounts to disregard of the Supreme Court's decision to release them temporarily and this is against the law." The commission added that "Delaying the trial of this case does not encourage revelation of the truth, be it for those who are detained or those who lodged their money in BACAR."[132] The Kagame government then seized BACAR and sold it without compensation. Kajeguhakwa and his two sons, who had already managed to escape Rwanda, were later convicted in absentia. But in a strange development a decade a later in 2012, Kajeguhakwa and his family returned to Rwanda and started new businesses under the name Energy Resources

132 The Rwanda National Commission of Human Rights, "Annual Report for the Year 2002," http://cndp.org.rw/fileadmin/user_upload/reports/Annual%20report%202002.pdf.

Petroleum Limited.[133] Nothing was ever mentioned about their lost businesses or the conviction in absentia. In Kagame's Rwanda, he is the law—he incarcerates and forgives at will.

The case of the Rwandan IT millionaire Miko Rwayitare was equally astonishing. When, in 2007, American investors in Rwanda's telephone company, Terracom/Rwandatel, attempted to sell shares to Rwayitare, the Kagame government would have none of it. Instead, the government seized the company, renationalized it, and shortly sold it to Libyans. The company soon collapsed and liquidated. The US ambassador to Rwanda, Michael Arietti, explained the saga as follows:

> Terracom descended from having a direct line to President Kagame to being vilified on the front pages of the local press. The GOR officially repurchased Terracom...Director General of the Rwanda Utility Regulatory Authority (RURA), Colonel Mudenge (Note: brother-in-law to Army Chief of Staff Major General James Kabarebe), threatened to "send in the troops to seize the company"...GOR continued to cite Wyler's mistakes including his attempt, in early 2006, to sell Terracom shares to business magnate Miko Rwayitare of CellTell as one of the main reasons for the nationalization of the company.[134]

---

133   http://www.theworldfolio.com/company/energy-resources-petroleum-limited-erp/1446/.

134   Ambassador Michael Ray Arietti, US Ambassador to Rwanda, "Foreign Investors in Rwanda: Perform or Get Out," Confidential, August 22, 2007, https://www.wikileaks.org/plusd/cables/07kigali754_a.html.

In 2013, the Union Trade Centre (UTC) Mall in Kigali, valued at US$20 million and owned by business mogul Tribert Rujugiro Ayabatwa, was seized by the Kagame government under the false pretext that it was "an abandoned asset." UTC was, of course, not abandoned—it was hosting eighty-one businesses, including top companies such as MTN Rwanda, Ethiopian Airlines, Access Bank, and Nakumatt Supermarket. More than four hundred Rwandans earned a living in these businesses. And then on August 24, 2015, the government pronounced UTC a tax defaulter. As explained in the US Department of State's 2015 Rwanda human-rights report, this development was bizarre because the government had seized UTC from Rujugiro two years earlier:

> Rwanda Revenue Authority stated businessman Tribert Rujugiro Ayabatwa was delinquent in paying taxes on the United Trade Center, a 144 billion Rwandan francs ($20 million) shopping mall. In 2013 the City of Kigali had seized ownership of the center, claiming it was an abandoned property due to Rujugiro's residency in self-imposed exile in South Africa.[135]

The story of UTC was to subsequently become even more peculiar. At the time of writing this book, the Kagame government was preparing to auction UTC. Having illegally seized

---

135 US Department of State, "Rwanda—Country Reports on Human Rights Practices 2015," 2016, https://www.state.gov/documents/organization/252929.pdf.

the company, and bankrupted it, the government was now ready to engage in further criminality—auction UTC.

On February 4, 2015, Assinapol Rwigara, considered one of Rwanda's leading business leaders, was killed in what was officially termed an accident. But Rwigara's family challenged the police version, instead pointing to possible murder. Shortly after, the government of Rwanda demolished Rwigara's hotel located near Kigali City Centre. The US Department of State's 2015 report on Rwanda explained the situation as follows:

> Following claims by the family of businessman Assinapol Rwigara that SSF killed Rwigara after a February 4 automobile accident, the City of Kigali seized real estate and in September demolished a hotel belonging to the Rwigara family. The City of Kigali claimed that the hotel had been built without proper permits and was structurally unsound; the family disputed the claim and provided copies of building permits to the press. The family claimed that the government and City of Kigali did not provide compensation for the loss of property and investment.[136]

Kagame's violence toward business is not limited to domestic enterprises. In my book *Kagame's Economic Mirage*, I demonstrate how foreign companies were illegally seized or denied a license to operate in Rwanda after investing substantial

136 Ibid.

capital. Foreign companies in that category included Chevron Corporation, Bakri International, Terracom, Vanoil Energy, Olyana Holdings, Natural Resources Development Company, and the African Development Corporation.[137]

In sharp contrast to the circumstances facing Rwandan top businesspeople, RPF's own companies are doing very well. RPF's conglomerate, Crystal Ventures Ltd (CVL), describes itself as a group that enters high-risk sectors with holdings that span "over various industries in and outside Rwanda." Estimated to be worth US$500 million, the group says that it employs more than twelve thousand workers.[138] Most of CVL's businesses are contracts with the Kagame government—especially road building and maintenance. A more appropriate name for Kagame's capitalism is crude cronyism, whereby a perfect marriage between the state and private special interests serves the well-connected RPF businesses. For the rest of the business sector, it is open season for seizure.

Kagame's socioeconomic success is a delusion of grandeur, as we have shown elsewhere.[139] Here, we summarize the economic reality of Kagame's Rwanda, beginning with the tininess of the formal sector. In the period June 2015–June 2016, for example, the total revenue collected in Rwanda was Rwf1 trillion—equivalent to US$1.2 billion.[140] By compari-

---

137   David Himbara, *Kagame's Economic Mirage* (North Charleston, SC: CreateSpace, 2016).

138   Crystal Ventures Ltd, http://www.crystalventuresltd.com/.

139   Himbara, *Kagame's Economic Mirage*.

140   Rwanda Revenue Authority, "Annual Report 2015/2016," http://www. rra.gov.rw/fileadmin/user_upload/rra_annualreport_2015-16_final.pdf.

son, foreign aid to Rwanda in 2015 was slightly over US$1 billion.[141] In other words, domestic revenue is larger than foreign aid by a slight margin. The domestic revenue remains meager because the Rwandan tax base has not significantly expanded since a decade ago. In 2015–2016, the number of taxpayers within the RRA taxpayer registry was 152,791, including private and public-sector entities, with a combined workforce of 303,550. Only 399 taxpayer/employers were defined as large—that is, an entity with one hundred or more workers. These numbers are dwarfed by the economically active population in Rwanda that is over six million. This means that only 303,550 Rwandans are employed in the formal economy, while 5.6 million are in subsistence agriculture or eking out a living in urban and rural informal sectors. Put in another way, 93 percent of Rwandan adults aged sixteen to sixty-five work outside the formal economy.

With these stark realities, it remains unclear how Kagame's Rwanda became an economic powerhouse. Will Kagame perform better at the continental level as he reforms the African Union? Do not bank on it.

---

141 The World Bank, "Net official development assistance and official aid received (current US$), 2015, http://data.worldbank.org/indicator/DT.ODA.ALLD.CD

CHAPTER 8

Genocide as Power

———

KAGAME'S POPULAR STORY ABOUT HIS role in Rwanda is simple. He stopped genocide. He pursued those who committed the Rwandan genocide in Congo where they had fled, taking with them more than a million people as human shields. He brought back the Rwandan refugees. He scattered the fighters among them deeper into DRC's forests. Meanwhile, he built a Rwandan economy that is now an African success story. Based on his success in Rwanda, Kagame is building the African Union, while keeping peace in the continent's conflict hot spots. This is a compelling story, endorsed by members of the global elite, including Bill Clinton, Tony Blair, and Ban Ki-moon. So why the violence that lingers on for twenty-three years? Why do Rwandans keep disappearing every year? From this work, we have learned several important lessons. Kagame became addicted to power, and more specifically, he became cripplingly hooked on the use of violence to accumulate and retain power. He learned that for violence to have the intended effect, it must be deployed on a massive scale, or it does not achieve its purpose. Violence must be so immense that only the insane may risk challenging it. And for overwhelming brutality to achieve its mission, there has to be a scapegoat, too. This way, his victims were frightened into total submission. Kibeho in Rwanda and Tingi Tingi in DRC illustrate irrational violence.

And yet, at another level, the violence we witness in Kagame's Rwanda has deeper Rwandan roots. Kagame's two predecessors suffered from the virus. Until he was overthrown in the 1973 military coup and his cabinet massacred by his successor, Grégoire Kayibanda could not give up violence and genocide as a means to power. He categorically refused to ratify the Genocide Convention. Kayibanda himself died under house arrest, in dire poverty. His cabinet ministers and senior officials were massacred. Then came the new autocrat, General Juvenal Habyarimana, who ruled Rwanda from 1973 until 1994. He, too, died violently when the aircraft in which he was traveling was shot down. Habyarimana signed the Genocide Convention but withheld the oversight responsibility of the International Court of Justice to try the perpetrators of genocide. Kagame used Habyarimana's legal maneuvering to deny the International Court of Justice to try him in a case filed by DRC for killing 3.5 million people. Kayibanda, Habyarimana, and Kagame share one critical characteristic besides their determination to cling to power. Each used genocide as means of intimidating and controlling the Rwandan population; each denied the International Court of Justice the right to take away the power to kill people.

From this legacy, we see that the use of violence and the crime of genocide is deeply entrenched into Rwanda's political psychology. This factor remains constant across regimes. Kagame, though, took these power tools to new levels. In this sense, Kagame's predecessors were, in comparison, mere amateurs. And this state of affairs does not appear to be ending shortly. Kagame, who has been in power for twenty-three years, changed the constitution to cling to power at least until 2034. And Article 114 of the Rwandan constitution Kagame engineered guarantees him freedom from accountability for life—or so he hopes. He might do well to remember the old Hegelian teaching that the only thing we learn from history is that we do not learn from history. Kagame's predecessor, Habyarimana, had named himself "Kinani," which translates into "the invincible."

BIBLIOGRAPHICAL NOTE

————

As NOTED IN THE PREFACE, this work is based exclusively on primary official documents, including reports of the governments of the United States, Rwanda, and the United Kingdom as well as reports of the United Nations, including the Security Council, the International Court of Justice, and the High Commission for Refugees. The cited RPF documents are found in the Security Council's archived materials. The bulk of the materials used in this book come from the US Department of State's annual reports on human-rights practices between 1994 and 2016. These sources are found in the footnotes in the text, together with links for reference purposes.